PRAISE FOR
AWAKE TO RIGHTEOUSNESS

"I want to highly recommend this amazing book, *Awake to Righteousness,* by my good friend Mark Greenwood. This book will reveal the heart of the Father to you and revelation knowledge to all who read it. God is supernatural, and we are called to live the supernatural life. There is a twenty-first century, new breed, prophetic company emerging in this generation that will rise far above the normal mindset of the day. This Daniel company will display incredible new miracles, healings, signs, and wonders through a "Love Reformation." They will break open revival in churches, cities, regions, and nations across the globe. They are filled with the power, life, and love of the Father that flow from a life rooted in the kingdom of God. If you are part of this new breed company and one of the hungry ones, then this book will serve as your preparatory guide to living a life of the miraculous."

Jeff Jansen
Senior Leader - Global Fire Church & Global Connect
Global Fire Ministries International
Author of *Glory Rising* and *Furious Sound of Glory*

"A common theme in so many Christian books and teachings these days is how to receive breakthrough, financial abundance, healing, and blessing. However, the wisdom of God says that if we were to seek first the kingdom of heaven and His righteousness, all these things would be added to us (Matthew 6:33). In *Awake to Righteousness*, Mark Greenwood addresses some common misunderstandings that have frustrated many of God's people from coming into their destiny, while he also expounds on the amazing and indescribable gift God says is already ours. I believe that when you read and meditate on the keys presented in this book, you will receive a powerful impartation, because I know that both Mark and his wife, Christine, live these truths out in a love-filled, glory-infused, and powerful life. Awake to righteousness!"

Todd Weatherly
Founder – Field of Dreams Australia

"I have had the privilege of journeying alongside Mark as he prayerfully and diligently crafted *Awake to Righteousness* from his heart onto these pages. Doing life in our church community with Mark, I also have the honor of seeing the consistent evidence of this revelation in his life, marriage, and ministry. I endorse this book with my whole heart because I see the fruit firsthand in Mark's life, and in the life of our community! The profound biblical truths systematically presented in *Awake to Righteousness* are not just theology, but an invitation into the unbridled intimacy with God you were created for."

David Ridley
Senior Leader – Glory City Church Darwin

"With remarkable biblical precision, Mark Greenwood, in his book *Awake to Righteousness,* joins theological intelligence with raw personal experience and revelation that honors the cross of Jesus and expounds on who we have become as the "righteousness of God" (2 Corinthians 5:21). With wisdom, Mark has crafted a book that invites us to know God and live from truth in a way that preserves the integrity of the gospel, resulting in personal transformation. You, as I was, will be moved in prayer as you read and discover the gift of righteousness given through Christ."

Adam Shepski
Global Prayer Catalyst
Youth for Christ International

"Awake to Righteousness contains the truth of the gospel that could change your life forever. I encourage you to read this book with a humble, open

heart and with the Holy Spirit. Take your time reading this book and wrestling through the pages. If there is something that challenges you or you disagree with while reading, open the Bible, and humbly, before the Lord, seek out the truth. I have met few people who carry biblical doctrine and humility hand in hand like Mark Greenwood. His hunger for the truth and his surrendered, laid-down life for Yeshua provoked me to reexamine the fullness of the gospel myself. The Holy Spirit awakened me to so much of the gospel I had not believed. *Awake to Righteousness* takes out the complexity and confusion so many people find in the gospel and presents it as it really is: simple and powerful! In fact, if you are not willing to receive it as a child, you might just miss it! Get ready to be transformed by the truth, fall more in love with God, and be overcome by the power of the good news!"

Jahleel Shelling
Celebrate Messiah Australia

"Awake to Righteousness lays the foundations of the gospel for all believers to have a true relationship with the Father and enjoy the freedom of their identity in Christ. By walking in these truths, we can fully embrace and fulfill the 'priesthood of all believers' mandate."

Carl Haasbroek,
Minister – Church of Christ Balaklava, SA

"With the news of Mark Greenwood's book *Awake to Righteousness*, I set time aside on a week-long fast to concentrate on reading the book in minute detail. I devoured every word and thought through every concept, illustration, and teaching. My conclusion: this book is not just nice to have; it is a necessary read. I believe this is the message that will set the church free. For too long, people have incorrectly believed they still have a 'bit of bad' in them, resigning themselves to the falsity that they can never be free and never overcome, that they are destined for a life of defeat. Mark's book confronts this lie, but in a way that is well researched, full of humility, and backed by sound biblical doctrine. For me, I have believed the teachings in Mark's book for some time; however,

Mark's book gave me the language to express what I believe. I highly recommend this book and believe it will be a book among books in the new generation of free Christian believers."

Daniel Zelli
CEO World Hope Network
Associate Pastor – Glory City Church Brisbane

"The purpose of salvation is to give us an individual and corporate confidence before God, to behold His glory and to rest in His presence; to know His voice and to learn His ways! *Awake to Righteousness* is a powerful instrument God will use to reinstate a holy confidence in His bride to draw near, with a true heart, in full assurance of faith (Hebrews 10:22). The days of a transactional type of relationship with the Father are over. It's time for genuine and true *interaction* with Him through the gift of righteousness! I believe the only way we will see a move of God's spirit that will abound in everlasting fruitfulness here on earth will be to embrace the true essence of the new covenant. 'None of them shall teach his neighbor, and none his brother, saying, "Know the Lord," for all shall know Me, from the least of them to the greatest of them'" (Hebrews 8:11).

Individually, from the least to the greatest, we will all know the Lord! Personal intimacy will be the new driving force for all God's sons and daughters! We will see freedom, diversity, and the presence of God flood every sphere of life as we boldly approach the throne of grace for help. I pray that you would not read this book to gather more information, but that you would allow Holy Spirit to draw you deep into a place of vulnerable and authentic relationship with God!"

Mitchell Ramsey
Co-founder – The Jesus School
Evangelist – Citipointe Church, Brisbane

AWAKE TO RIGHTEOUSNESS

A LIFE-CHANGING LOOK
AT THE SUBSTANCE OF SALVATION

MARK GREENWOOD
FOREWORD BY KATHERINE RUONALA

DEDICATION

For Jesus, my King and my best friend, thank you for showing me the way to the Father, and for reconciling me to Him through your death and resurrection. I am overwhelmed by your affection for me. I know you and I desire to know you infinitely more. May your bride become everything you have dreamed of for eternity past. I love you. You have my whole heart.

For Christine, my perfect wife, to journey in righteousness and love with you is the greatest gift of my life. Your constant support and belief in me is astounding.

Thank you for seeing me just as He does. I love you.

*"And this righteousness will bring peace.
Yes, it will bring quietness and confidence forever."*

ISAIAH 32:17

TABLE OF CONTENTS

FOREWORD

Romans 14:17 tells us the kingdom of God is "righteousness and peace and joy in the Holy Spirit." Righteousness is key to our kingdom experience. People generally understand and desire to walk in supernatural peace and joy, but without Holy Spirit giving us a revelation of righteousness, we cannot experience true peace. When we don't experience the reality of being set free from shame and guilt, the fear of not measuring up will consistently rob us of peace and prevent us from experiencing true, unbridled joy. Knowing the truth of righteousness and how to walk it out in faith in our everyday lives is essential to living in true freedom, peace, and joy in the Holy Ghost!

Awake to Righteousness brings wonderful light and language to this life-changing truth, challenging believers to be the just who "live by faith" (Galatians 3:11). Mark is a personal friend, and it has been a delight and privilege to dialogue with him and observe his genuine humility and continual, committed pursuit of truth. His gifts and intelligence are without question, and his character testifies to the uncompromising commitment he and his wife, Christine, have to walking these truths out.

The fruit of this message is abundantly clear, and it is fruit that remains. Mark's work among indigenous Australians has been remarkable, with whole communities being impacted by the power of this glorious truth. Mark and Christine were willing to joyfully pay the price to disciple and

1

empower two or three in remote areas of the Northern Territory, and as the message of righteousness transformed lives, those disciples made disciples, until whole communities were touched and many saved. Mark's influence as a teacher is now being felt and recognized across the nation through his writings, Youth for Christ ministries like "The Jesus School," and church leadership in his hometown. As churches and leaders are embracing the move of Holy Spirit, the nation is rapidly awakening to righteousness.

This book will refresh your heart, and the message of freedom it carries will challenge and inspire. I am excited for those who will read it, and it is my sincere prayer you, too, will "awake to righteousness" and experience the peace and joy that follows.

Katherine Ruonala
Author of *Living in the Miraculous*, among others
Senior Leader – Glory City Church, Brisbane, and the Glory City Network (GCN)
Founder and Facilitator – Australian Prophetic Council

ACKNOWLEDGEMENTS

Christine Greenwood – My wife. You are my constant encouragement and my best friend. You are a fighter for the truth in your life and in the lives of many others. I pray that the deep desires of your heart, that I and the Father alone have seen, continue to become a manifest reality in your life. Thank you for tirelessly supporting me in the pursuit of my destiny in Him. Thank you for seeing me. Thank you for leading me to Jesus all those years ago, by the manifest grace of God you showed me in my brokenness. You are embarrassingly empowering in many ways, to many people.

Katherine Ruonala – You are not just an apostolic influencer of nations, or my leader alone, but my friend. It is the things you do that no one sees, the jealous care you have for my family, the long conversations, the insightful advice, the confronting humility, the tireless passion you have for people to know the Father, your correction where necessary, and your love toward me that will speak into eternity. Your empowerment and trust in me has been incredible. Thank you for believing in my ability to teach this gospel message and for drawing it more accurately out of me at every turn. I am truly privileged to serve the Lord under your leadership.

David Ridley, Caleb Bowles, and Mitchell Ramsey – Three key friends and brothers who have sought to practice, preach, and multiply the gospel across our globe, with a mutual submission to one another out of reverence for Christ. Thank you for believing in me, holding me to the truth at all times, and never changing the subject. I could never have imagined doing the things we have done together with God, nor the things we are yet to do. Without you three, there would be no book. My name is on the cover, but it is our collective, refining relationships that have brought so much life and clarity to the words within these pages. I pray that we would stand firm, arm in arm, for the faith of the gospel, for the rest of our lives.

Jeff Jansen – Thank you for being a faithful mouthpiece for Father God and for your encouragement of my destiny in Him. Your insight into my destiny has held my focus on occasions during the writing of this book. Also, thank you for being down to earth and available. I am grateful for the sacrifices you have made to lead people deeper into the realm of the Father and the heart of His love.

Todd and Rachel Weatherly – You incite far more than you know on the earth. You are a connection point for so many lines to cross in the bride, cultivating an apostolic unity in profound ways. You have pumped the life of God into our nation for years. Your love for my wife and I is humbling. You really are a "don't argue" kind of couple! When well-roundedness or wisdom from above comes up in our conversations, your names usually come up as an example of both. Thank you for bringing health to so many and for pursuing at great cost the things heaven declares over our nation and the nations.

Todd White and Dan Mohler – We are yet to meet, but you are the two men through whom the message of my sonship came to me. I was a broken and tormented Christian before I was confronted with your declaration of real freedom. I am forever grateful for your decision to believe, live, and preach the gospel fearlessly and without pretence. You are both sacrificial catalysts for global transformation. You will never fully know the extent and impact your lives are having in our generation. Thank you abundantly, on behalf of the many you have met and impacted, and also the multitudes whom you may never know.

I also acknowledge – The Greenwood family (Greens), thank you for raising me in the way I should go, and encouraging me to pursue the Father. I cannot thank you enough; the Pereiras, for your incredible support, constant love, and faithfulness; the Glory City Church family in Darwin, Brisbane, and the network around the world; the Youth for Christ Australia family; Bunumbirr and Vanessa Marika (Yolngu for Jesus); Kata Majetic, my beloved sister; Jason and Olive Tarau; Ruth Ridley; Chloe Bowles; Stu and Kara Bolger; the West family and my sister Ana; Adam Shepski; Ben Fitzgerald and Daniel Hagen, for your hearts for awakening and for all that you are pioneering around the globe; Leon and Sonja Bowles and the Exchange Church community; Joel and Candace Shaw; Daniel Zelli for your thoughtful advice and encouragement; Carl Haasbroek, for faithfully carrying a legacy of righteousness and being a Papa bear by the Spirit; Nathaniel and Hayley Oliveri; Joel and Savannah Ramsey; Roger and Vivienne Latham (we treasure you Mama and Papa of the NT); Jahleel Shelling; Liam Swaine; the incredible Jesus School leadership team; Darren Steen; Shane and Christy Rayner; Len and Heather Magee; and so many more who have inspired and encouraged me in the Lord. I appreciate you all more than you know. Thank you all for your faithful friendship and your input into my life. Thank you for believing the gospel and making a way for multitudes to know the Father. Space here limits me from expressing the depth of my gratitude to you all.

INTRODUCTION

"Awake to righteousness, and do not sin;
for some do not have the knowledge of God."

1 CORINTHIANS 15:34 NKJV

Once upon a time, there was a chicken named Will. Will was pecking around the chicken coop one day and found an old letter. Will had never seen this letter and read it excitedly. As he did his heart jumped, because it explained it was possible for a chicken to be supernaturally transformed into an eagle.

There had always been a desire in Will's heart to be an eagle, but he'd never thought it would be possible in his life. That night Will prayed to God and believed it was possible for him to be born again into an eagle. As Will prayed, a bolt of lightning struck him, and he immediately became a fully-fledged eagle!

The crazy thing was that Will was so used to his experience of being a chicken, he didn't realize he had become an eagle, even though the old letter had promised he would. From then on he walked around the coop acting and pecking like a chicken, but all the while he was an eagle. It became difficult for Will to still act like a chicken because he was no longer designed for that life. He no longer enjoyed pecking around for food and scraps like he

7

used to. He became more and more dissatisfied with his condition but could not put his claw on the issue. He continued to ask God to make him more like an eagle, but never changed and lost hope. This went on for some time until one day, a majestic eagle flew over Will's chicken coop and saw the funny sight of an eagle acting like a chicken.

The eagle swooped down and perched on a tree next to the coop. The eagle yelled out to Will, "What are you doing down there in that coop acting like a chicken?"

"What do you mean?" Will replied, "I am a chicken."

The eagle laughed at Will and said, "Come, spread your wings and fly with me. You are an eagle just like me." Will didn't have time to think as the eagle flew away. He spread what he thought were his chicken wings and saw two broad eagle wings. With three strong flaps, some faith, and courage, Will flew high above the chicken coop and soared as eagles do.[1]

What if far more happened to us on the cross than we realize? What if the cross was never meant to represent a future hope of heaven to us, but rather a completely transformed life here on earth? What if eternity itself, being united with the Father, begins at our conversion and not at our death?

This story of the chicken and the eagle expresses the heart of the message of this book. Too many of us are stuck in a chicken coop of guilt, shame, condemnation, and unfulfilled dreams of greatness. This creates an identity crisis that keeps us behaving like the chickens we *think* we are.

- Do you feel stuck on a hamster wheel of do-to-be Christianity, trying to please a God you think is distant and displeased?

- Are you are experiencing ongoing and frustrating bondage to sin?

- Do you suffer from spiritual or emotional instability and fear?

- Are you ruled by guilt, shame, condemnation, or self-consciousness?

- Are you experiencing a barrier to enjoying real intimacy with God?

- Are you looking for satisfaction in your Christian walk that you have not found?

- Do you feel you are missing out on the consistent, abundant life promised by Jesus (John 10:10)?

If you answered yes to any of these, welcome to your wake-up call. Prepare to be equipped in freedom and to live a transformed life. Prepare to awake to righteousness.

This book is about righteousness: God's provision of our new nature in Christ and the wide-open door to knowing the Father. It changes every area of our lives. Its ultimate purpose is an intimacy with God and with each other that transforms the world around us. We must never change the subject from knowing God and making Him known. As we will see, this is the heart of the gospel.

An awakening is increasingly covering the globe. I am a privileged participant, and equally a spectator, as it grows in influence and impact around Australia—through a variety of ministries—by the power of Holy Spirit. Evidence of this can also be found all over the world through many people and movements. It is an awakening to intimacy with God through His righteousness, freely imparted to us in Christ. It is a rediscovery of what Christian salvation is and what it means. It is a priesthood movement of sons and daughters walking with the Father and functioning powerfully in the Son. Thousands are coming to the Lord as it gradually spills further out of the churches and into society. It is a surge of Jesus people in the twenty-first century, passionate to advance the kingdom of heaven in a sustainable, holistic way. The magnetic presence of a person who knows God and rightly discerns his new nature in Him, with additional signs, wonders, and a holy life, is drawing multitudes to the King of kings!

As the awakening continues, and multitudes adjust to a doctrinal foundation of righteousness by which to relate to God and live the intended Christian life, I have felt stirred and invited by God to write this book. My heart is to make the message accessible, practical, and incorruptible, by His grace. In spite of doubts I could even accomplish this task, I have obeyed God's invitation, trusting the necessary capacity and clarity always accompanies His invitations when we faithfully walk in them. Finding this to be abundantly true, I believe this book has become what He intended, and it will accomplish what He desires.

In explaining the message of righteousness and some key topics it forces a fresh look at, I divided this into three parts:

PART ONE – "DEAD TO SINNER"

We will examine the "sinner saved by grace" idea scripturally and practically. In the same way Will is no longer a chicken, we are no longer sinners. We will look at:

- The "sinner saved by grace" oxymoron,
- How it is scripturally impossible that we remain sinners after conversion,
- How Christ eradicated our old, sinful nature,
- What it truly means to be born again, and
- My personal awakening.

To fully understand what you are in Christ, it helps to understand what you *are not*. The limitations the "sinner saved by grace" mantra has produced in the church in recent generations is devastating, most of all because of the hindrance to intimacy with God and the expectation for an inescapably sinful lifestyle it can create. It is time for a new and unwavering global stance in the church on the essential definition of Christians, and the true substance of salvation.

PART TWO – THE RIGHTEOUSNESS OF GOD IN CHRIST

In part two, we will explore the definition and reality of righteousness as our new nature in Christ, our access to God, and the practical ramifications this has for our lives. This includes:

- Righteousness: Sharing God's righteousness in Christ,

- A divine "inventory" of the redeemed man. Discovering the new you,

- The deceitfulness of sin: A biblical look at what sin is, where it comes from, and how to live free from it when it is no longer in your nature,

- A missing link between our new nature and our manifest freedom, and how to bridge the gap,

- The reality of Jesus's life as our ultimate example and reference for what our new lives can look like, and

- Intimacy with God—*the whole point*. Righteousness is the door to the relationship with God we have always desired.

PART THREE – CRITICAL CLARITY

Righteousness gives you a new set of "glasses" for seeing the Christian life. Once you understand it, you understand many things differently. Looking at foundational concepts of the Christian life, part three will answer questions that commonly arise for those exploring the truth of righteousness. You will find, as I have, that righteousness is an incorruptible doctrine. We will explore:

- The will and nature of God revealed in Christ,

- What grace is,

- How to rightly divide the word of truth,

- Who the Romans 7 man is,

- If Christians are already sanctified,

- A brief history of righteousness and some seasons in time where it was forgotten or misunderstood, and

- Some things the "finished work" is not.

If, by the time you finish reading this book, you have a new doctrinal stance or language, but no more closeness to the Father or manifest holiness, than either I have failed to communicate properly, or you have misunderstood the "why" behind this message. This book is an invitation for intimacy with God, not mere intellectual stimulation. It is for a transformed life, not a transformed lingo. The best way to view the doctrine presented in this book is to be open to cultivating an intimate living room, creating space and freedom for you to delve deep into the relationship with Father God that you desire.

I have sought to write this book in a place of closeness to God with my ear to His chest. This closeness to my Father is the reason for this book and my life. It is the thing I would die for and the thing I live for. Intimacy is God's motive for establishing the new covenant, and the reason for our salvation. My prayer is that you would respond in like manner. The true "fight of faith" every Christian is ultimately engaged in is a fight for intimacy with God, not an activity *for* God. Authentic activity will become the spontaneous result of this intimacy. The devil knows this well, making our relationship with the Father the most targeted and attacked aspect of our lives. It is time for the church to become deeply familiar with the Father. It is time we became familiar with ourselves in Christ. To know Him in a real way is not an elusive anomaly. It is not a distant hope, dreamed about only through a great divide of incompatibility. Our new life in the Godhead is God's greatest desire and most freely-given gift!

It is time to leave the chicken coop. It is time to fly, as eagles do. Come on an incredible adventure. Get acquainted with the Father through your likeness to His Son, Jesus. We must finally walk in our compatibility with

God so we can reveal the will and nature of God to the world—a world desperately searching for the Father.

(ENDNOTES)

1. David Ridley, "The Chicken and the Eagle" (The Jesus School booklet, Youth for Christ Australia, 2015).

PART ONE
DEAD TO 'SINNER'

CHAPTER 1

THE GREAT OXYMORON

Oxymoron - "A figure of speech in which
apparently contradictory terms appear in conjunction."[1]

Seriously funny	*Jumbo shrimp*
Living dead	*Genuine imitation*
Alone together	*Original copies*

Oxymorons are commonly used to emphasize a contradiction in a humorous way, often found in hyperbolic writing. Why the English lesson? Because some oxymorons are no laughing matter; one, in particular, exists to describe a fundamentally flawed Christian belief. Unfortunately, because of some grave misunderstandings in the church for a few centuries, many have been using the following oxymoron to define themselves as Christians:

Sinner saved

A common Christian description for the condition of the believer is "sinner saved by grace." This is an oxymoron. If you have been a Christian for more than a year, then no doubt you have heard this term before and possibly associate yourself with it.

After many years of living my Christian life as this oxymoron, I was shocked to discover the term "sinner" is never used in Scripture to describe the nature of Christians. A Christian "sinner saved by grace" is not even alluded to in the Bible. Yes, you read that correctly. This may be a surprise to many who read this book. If this statement is a shock, don't worry, we will explore this conclusively.

There is a drastic change of terminology taking place in the church, enabling a drastic change of life.

We must not fall into a dangerous trap of defining the condition of our nature by our thoughts, feelings, actions, or experiences. These are a significant source of our mistaken terminology, along with a couple of misinterpretations from Scripture. We must only look at what Scripture says we are, and either agree or disagree with the truth. It remains the truth either way, but it will only change our experience when we understand and set our faith on it.

We cannot be *sinners* and simultaneously be *saved*. This is because sin was precisely the thing we were saved from when we believed the gospel. We are sinners *or* we are saved. Anything else is a contradiction, an oxymoron.

If this book is your first introduction to this understanding of the gospel, then embracing this message will require humility and openness. The possible Scripture passages spinning through your head right now objecting to my above statements have simple explanations, which we will look at together. Have you believed and behaved as though you are a sinner all this time? It might hurt a little as the truth sinks in that you did not have to. For me, it was like having a winning lottery ticket in my pocket for years, then fighting over scraps and *experiencing* poverty because I did not know I had the ticket. This is a liberating discomfort, I promise. I ask that you would persevere with this and consider the Scriptures presented throughout the book objectively and prayerfully.

I know of multiple ministers who have come into contact with the truth of righteousness. Many spend long seasons preaching that we are sinners, often with a natural progression of misguided doctrines based on this theology. When they discover the scriptural soundness of righteousness and the personal liberty the message enables, they are courageous enough to ditch the oxymoron. Some, who previously had their identity tied up in their positions, are no longer defined by this because the intimacy they have discovered with the Father through righteousness now defines them. I am deeply inspired when I see this happen. Righteousness is a scripturally incorruptible message. There is nothing new or modern about it. It is just the gospel, understood in its true simplicity and with clarity, having real results in our lives. Because most ministers honor the integrity of the Scriptures above their reputation, countless leaders are waking up to righteousness. Most ministers of the gospel do their work with absolute purity of heart. They have a fundamental motive to see others do well in their faith. They are often willing to be wrong if it means drastic liberty for the people they care for so deeply.

I had to have my hands pried off my long-held "sinner" paradigm. I had spent years learning and even teaching the wrong things about who we are as Christians. I went through Bible college and did huge amounts of personal study, hungry for a relationship with God and to know the truth. Because of my fundamental misunderstanding, despite the great things I gained through this season, I ended up with a sense He was further away from me than when I began.

The truth ultimately poked at my deep, unquenched thirst for real freedom from sin and for true intimacy with God, finally reaching a degree where I was humbled, learned the truth, and then was set free. Romans 7 (chapter 14) and other hindrances slowly fell away as I learned the plain context of these passages.

I once found my identity in my ability to learn and teach theology, somehow blinded to the reality I did not *know* God. I also did not live a life I felt was worth reproducing by making disciples (Matthew 23:15). I now have the privilege of sharing this message with many, with the testimony of a transformed life and the doctrinal insight to reproduce the power of that transformation. I will share my story throughout the book.

If you learn and believe the truth found only in Scripture, it will set you free (John 8:32). If you disagree or remain ignorant, then the wrong conclusions you make will keep you in bondage (2 Peter 1:9). Simple, isn't it? Scary too. What you think you are will determine how you behave. Belief determines behavior, but only Scripture will reveal your true nature and identity.

Here is the simple truth about us that we will now unpack together:

> *We were sinners. Grace saved us from our sin.*
> *We are now the righteousness of God in Christ*

This is the message of this book. As you will see, this truth changes everything.

"BEHOLD, THE LAMB OF GOD, WHO TAKES AWAY THE SIN OF THE WORLD."

Every rational Christian believes God hates sin. Many, however, have not considered that He hates it so much, He made a way for the *nature* of sin to be taken out of us at the cross, making way for true freedom and real intimacy with the Father. Let's look at a profound passage of Scripture, teaching us we are not oxymorons.

There was no greater person in the old covenant than John the Baptist (Matthew 11:11). His entire life purpose was to "make straight the path of the Lord" (John 1:23), to announce, baptize, and usher Jesus into His earthly ministry. John the Baptist knew his purpose. He was symbolic of the decrease of the old covenant and of Jesus being the beginning of the new covenant, hence John's comment that he must decrease and Jesus must increase (John 3:30). (Based on this context, this is not an accurate comment for Christians to make of themselves. We are not called to decrease, but to consider ourselves dead indeed to sin and alive to God in Christ Jesus as Romans 6:11 teaches, but we will get to this.) The climax of John's life was his opportunity to baptize Jesus. He had preached repentance, baptized many, and spoken of the coming Messiah as he waited for his promised visit from Him.

One day John saw Jesus coming toward him as he was baptizing. I imagine his heart skipped a beat and time seemingly slowed down as he realized who this was. John made his long-awaited statement that introduced the incarnate Son of God to the world, the overflow of the meditation of his heart about the reason he knew Jesus would come into the world. He summed it all up in one profound sentence:

> *"Behold, the Lamb of God,*
> *who takes away the sin of the world!"*
> **JOHN 1:29**

John knew enough about sin to be preaching repentance from it. He also compelled people to live differently as evidence of repentance (Matthew 3:8). We also learn from John's statement above that he knew enough about sin to know it had to be eradicated and taken away from us. Otherwise, we would never be free from sin under the law (Galatians 3:11; Romans 3:20). If his baptism for repentance was doing the trick of dealing with sin effectively, he would not have excitedly stated that the Lamb of God would *take away* the sins of the world. Repentance was part of our answer, but it was not the whole answer. We required a repentance that led to *regeneration*—to have the old, sinful nature taken away and a whole new nature received. This is the thing Jesus came to purchase for us. This was His mission. Here is a powerful statement to remember regarding the purpose of the atonement of Christ:

> *Jesus saved us from our sin, not in our sin.*

We learn by John's statement that Jesus had not come to save us *in* our sin, but to save us *from* our sin. The Lamb of God *takes away* our sin. He does not leave it in us. Our sinful nature was the thing which made us incompatible with God. It was also the reason we could not live consistently holy lives. Adam inherited a sinful nature when He believed Satan's lies in the garden, giving up the image and likeness of God to take on a fallen nature infused with sin (Genesis 1:26–27, 3:1–6). We are all born into Adam's state as a result, with a sinful nature like the one he developed. We must now all be born again to have that sinful nature removed in Christ.

To term ourselves as sinners saved by grace misunderstands John's informative statement and confuses the purpose of Christ's atoning work.

> *Jesus's death on the cross did not offer us a more permanent covering for our sinful condition; it removed the sin nature we were in bondage to.*

Jesus never came to provide a more permanent *covering* than the old covenant sacrificial system could provide, but rather to enable an actual *removal* of our sins. Jesus purchased us *from* sin and *for* Him, in a more unfathomable way than we ever could have imagined.

MISDIAGNOSED AND MISTREATED

In his famous letter to the church in Rome, Paul said to "consider yourselves *dead to sin* and *alive to God* in Christ Jesus" (Romans 6:11, emphasis mine). I don't know about you, but for many years of my Christian life, I did the opposite. I considered myself *alive* to sin and *distant* from God and Christ Jesus! This simple misunderstanding caused huge issues in my life.

When we misdiagnose ourselves as sinners, we mistreat
ourselves as those who are distant from
and disapproved by God.

I used to read of powerful concepts and possibilities in the Scriptures, but apply them to "special" or "anointed" people and not to myself. I would browse the many promises in Scripture about the glorious life available but separate myself from having access to them, because I failed to see who I had *become* in Christ. I perpetually gave in to the idea I could not attain these glorious truths, or they were all reserved for a future time, but I was called to strive for them nonetheless. Because of this, my spiritual life became a steady mix of unfulfilled desires, guilt, shame, and condemnation.

I would read in the Gospels about the incredible life of Jesus, but not believe I could live the way He lived, thinking He did not have a sinful nature like the one I believed I still had. *How can I do what He did when I am so different from the way He was?* I would think. Jesus's disciples had sinful natures, however, so I defined myself by their actions instead. Jesus is the Christian example though, not the disciples (1 Peter 2:21).

As *Jesus* is "so also are we in this world" (1 John 4:17), not as Peter was. If we say we abide in Jesus, we "ought to walk in the same way in which he walked" (1 John 2:6), not as James and John walked (more on this in chapter 9).

Understanding our righteousness in Christ unlocks the kingdom for us (Matthew 6:33). It reveals what we have inherited as sons and daughters of God. We must rightly see what happened on the cross. We learn that Jesus, on our behalf, achieved many things we still can *feel* we need to achieve. Once we understand this, then we can get on with living an empowered life of freedom and fellowship with God.

The extent to which we have mistreated ourselves in our misdiagnosed state is huge. We are called to be the powerful and victorious bride of Christ, modeling what true holiness and wisdom from above can do on the earth. We are called to heal the broken, set the captives free, and reconcile people to the Father by exhibiting His love in our lives. But how can we set captives free if we still believe we are captives to sin?

Faith is designed to empower our understanding.

Faith empowers the things we believe about ourselves. When our understanding is that we are natural sinners, we will produce the appropriate lifestyle to this belief, reinforcing our wrong understanding as our experience continues to complement it. Scripture enables us to *challenge* our experience by *changing* our perspective of ourselves to the perspective God has of us. I am talking about actual, *experiential* freedom. True freedom is produced by thinking differently about who we are.

If you believe you are a dog, then will you think twice before barking at the mailman? Of course not, your thoughts about yourself determine and justify your actions. In the same way, when you think you remain a sinner after conversion, you will never believe you can live free from sin. You will also read Scripture through the lens of your perceived identity. You will limit yourself from looking to Jesus as your example, making Him an unattainable standard you will never reach, instead excusing your sinful behaviors with a misguided understanding of His grace.

If you believe you are destined to a life of struggle with sin, then your faith is limited to that experience.

What if you find out you are a saint? What if you find out you are holy? What if you find out Jesus is not an unreachable example to compare yourself to but, in fact, He is the mirror in which you discover your new self? Well, if it is *actually* true, and if you agree your new self is who you are in a place of intimacy, Holy Spirit will empower it to become your experience by His grace.

A MISPLACED HATRED

"The fear of the Lord is hatred of evil."
PROVERBS 8:13

To fear God is a profound but often misunderstood thing. It means to revere, honor, and submit to God in awe, the way He deserves, by nature of His perfection and power. As you come to know Him, both as intimate Father and almighty God, enjoying His nature of unrelenting love, you will discover in yourself a certain hatred of things opposing His glorious character and design for your life. That is why authentic fear of the Lord leads to the hatred of evil. As Christians, we have no problem understanding we are called to turn away from evil when it's understood as sinful behavior. Throughout church history, we have turned away from an expression of evil and maintained a certain purity of behavior, or at least an intention of purity.

The problem, though, is we have largely failed to identify ourselves by the life and nature of Jesus after we believe. We do not view ourselves as those He has conformed to *His* image, nor do we see ourselves as having had our sinful nature removed (Romans 8:29; 1 John 4:17; 2 Peter 1:4). When we truly understand this, it naturally transforms our behavior. Instead of defining ourselves by Scripture alone, we have let the things we experience, think, and feel dictate who we are.

We have forgotten the simple reason God became a man in the first place: to remove our sinful nature and unite us in the Godhead.

For hundreds of years, in many churches, we have taught that we, as God's children, are still essentially evil. We think we have succeeded in the hatred of evil as Proverbs 8 invites us to, but we have wrongly identified our nature by this evil *instead.* Let that sink in. This contradiction is being rapidly exposed in the church. It is our greatest ever, albeit unintentional, slap in the face to a loving Father.

He paid precious blood to set us free from the very thing we continue to claim is our essence.

If the fear of the Lord is to hate evil, then what could be worse than believing we still have a sinful, evil nature? When we do this, we are nurturing and making exceptions for evil to remain among us, not hating it. There are forty-seven uses of the words "sinners" or "sinner" in the New Testament Scriptures. If we look through each of these occurrences, we will find that none refer to the nature of people who have come to a saving faith in Jesus. The Greek word used for sinner in the Bible *(hamartōlos)*[2] means, "pre-eminently sinful, especially wicked." Hardly a term I want to associate with if it is no longer my biblical definition as a Christian.

But didn't Paul say he was the chief of sinners? you may be wondering. Yes, he did (1 Timothy 1:15). This verse has caused great confusion for Christians when they refer to themselves by the term sinner, especially as it is the only Bible verse where a Christian seems to use the term to define himself. When you look at the passage in context, and at the Greek word used for "chief" *(prōtos),*[3] you will see Paul is proclaiming the enormity of God's mercy toward his *former* sinful life, not stating his current definition as a Christian.

Another word used in English translations for the word chief is "foremost" or "first." This is a lot like if you were to win a math competition in high school and then no one broke your winning record for the next twenty years. You would remain the chief mathematician of that school, even though this title refers to an achievement from twenty years earlier. Paul was the "foremost" or the first of sinners, a more accurate take on the word "prōtos." He was saying, "I hold first place as a prior sinner and no one beats my record. If God can have mercy on me, he can have mercy on anyone!" Paul was exemplifying the mercy of God shown for such a former blasphemer; he was not making a case for Christians to be titled sinners. When considering the heart of the entire passage, you will see Paul was referencing his old life as an example, not his current life, explicitly using his past actions as the example for his sinfulness (1 Timothy 1:13). One quick look at the apostle's life reinforces this. His behavior was dramatically transformed after his encounter with Jesus on the road to Damascus. He lived a powerfully holy life as an example for the church. Reading the entire first chapter of 1 Timothy with this in mind, you see how it fits together.

The danger of believing we are still sinners, apart from it not being scriptural, is it robs us from feeling adequate enough to have deep intimacy with God, the thing He created us for. It keeps us stuck in guilt, shame, and condemnation: things we'd never have to deal with again if we would only see what He did on that cross and learn to live in His resurrection life.

We must awake to righteousness and "not go on sinning" (1 Corinthians 15:34). It is time to ditch the oxymoron and draw a line in the sand for true purity and the finished work of Jesus in our lives.

(ENDNOTES)

1. *Concise Oxford English Dictionary* (New York: Oxford University Press, 2011).
2. James Strong, *The New Strong's Exhaustive Concordance of the Bible: Classic Edition* (Edinburgh: Thomas Nelson, 1852), G0268
3. Strong's G4413.

CHAPTER 2

THE OLD IS GONE (AND SO IS THE MIDDLE)

MISTAKEN APPEARANCES

News flash! The second appearance of Jesus will not remove our sinful nature from us, nor will it regenerate us to our intended design. Why? Because His first appearance did!

I believe in the second bodily appearance of Jesus at the end of the age. However, the *purpose* of His return needs clarifying. There has been a serious case of mistaken appearances in some theology. We have considered our redemption from sin as something that remains a future event. Sure, we will put off our earthly tent and receive glorified bodies.

We will dwell in the new earth and see the end of every remnant of man's fall that still impacts the earth today. We also are growing in revelation, relationship with God, and love. But the contents of our earthly tent have been transformed. It was during Jesus's first appearance when our old, sinful nature was put to death and we were recreated in His glorious nature. That is why the writer of Hebrews could say:

> *"So Christ, having been offered once to bear the sins of many,*
> *will appear a second time, not to deal with sin but to save those*
> *who are eagerly waiting for him."*
> **HEBREWS 9:28**

Why won't Jesus deal with sin at His second appearance? Because His first appearance dealt with it—He bore our sins for us and destroyed them in His death, putting the old, sinful nature away. We must no longer associate with the old man all over again by remaining in a "sinner saved by grace" paradigm. This can become our personal reality when we put our faith in Jesus. If we mistake the purpose of His appearances, then we will also mistakenly ignore Jesus's saving work in our lives and act as though what He did was only for a future time. This is a crippling conclusion, which made my spiritual life difficult for years.

The second appearance occurs when Jesus returns for His already blood-bought, spotless bride. His second appearance will not fulfill God's redemption plan and remove sin from us. His return is for those already regenerated into his likeness (Hebrews 10:14; 2 Peter 1:4)—those already formed in the righteousness of the Father the moment they were reborn (2 Corinthians 5:21). We may learn to live in and express the fullness of this righteousness as we grow in intimacy and truth, but it still exists inside us now as the divine attribute of our new nature in Christ. (We will unpack this more in part 2.)

Because of these mistaken appearances, we have lived with an "ambiguous middle" or "halfway" mindset. We define ourselves as both "saved and being saved," or "simultaneously sinners and saints." This is not true, and it robs Jesus of the thing he came to purchase us for—real freedom from sin, powerful kingdom lives, and true intimacy with God, all made possible by our likeness to Him. Jesus took sin out of us once and for all: Christ *"offered for all time a single sacrifice for sins"* (Hebrews 10:12).

CO-CRUCIFIED AND CO-RESURRECTED

How did Jesus accomplish this mission to set us free from the sin nature? It is called co-crucifixion and co-resurrection. He paid for our real transition from the old, sinful nature. Our death with Christ to the old, sinful nature is not theoretical, philosophical, or positional. It is *real*.

We must realize His death was our death too.

These verses show you are not slowly dying to the old man, but you *died* to him completely when you were crucified with Christ.

> *"We know that our old self was crucified with him in order*
> *that the body of sin might be brought to nothing, so that we*
> *would no longer be enslaved to sin."*
> **ROMANS 6:6**

> *"For you have died, and your life is hidden with Christ in God."*
> **COLOSSIANS 3:3**

> *"I have been crucified with Christ. It is no longer I who live, but*
> *Christ who lives in me. And the life I now live in the flesh I live by*
> *faith in the Son of God, who loved me and gave himself for me."*
> **GALATIANS 2:20**

*"In him also you were circumcised with a circumcision made
without hands, by putting off the body of the flesh, by the
circumcision of Christ, having been buried with him in baptism, in
which you were also raised with him through faith in the powerful
working of God, who raised him from the dead."*
COLOSSIANS 2:11–12

This is the simple message of Christ and Him crucified that possessed the apostle Paul (1 Corinthians 2:2). He preached nothing but this message because he knew Jesus's death was also *our* death and His resurrection is where our new life begins. He understood this reality could reach far into our lives, creating the most empowered and liberated Christian experience for all who believe.

THE OLD IS GONE

*"Therefore, if anyone is in Christ, he is a new creation. The old
has passed away; behold, the new has come."*
2 CORINTHIANS 5:17

Our lives and experiences, reinforced by our misdiagnoses that Christians are sinners, have brought many of us to a conclusion of an ambiguous middle. This idea is that somehow due to an experience of sin in our lives, we remain somewhere in the middle of Adam and Christ, between unholy and holy—even though the Bible tells us blatantly that in Christ the old man (sinful nature) has gone (Romans 6:6; Colossians 2:11, 3:3; 2 Corinthians 5:17, 21; Galatians 2:20, 5:24).

We have sadly concluded we are simultaneously "saved and being saved," or "sinner and saint." The Bible presents no such middle ground. Nowhere in Scripture will you be told you still have a sinful nature after Christ comes to live in you, or that you are somewhere between Adam and Christ, on a journey from A to B. As we have seen, we are not dying to the old man; we died to him when we shared in Christ's death. The "middle ground" idea is a dangerous and confusing one to live in.

> *Our "ambiguous middle" understanding gives place for an
> "ambiguous middle" experience.*

God compels us to "not be unequally yoked with unbelievers. For what partnership has righteousness with lawlessness?" (2 Corinthians 6:14). Surely He has not caused His Son to be unequally yoked to a half-holy bride. Light has *no* fellowship with darkness. Frankly, to relate to God in a compatible relationship requires us to become like He is (1 John 4:17; 2 Corinthians 5:21; 2 Peter 1:4), or for Him to become as we were. I cannot imagine what the world would look like if the latter was the case and He had become a sinner! Aren't you glad we are the ones who were changed by the crucifixion and resurrection of Christ, not Him?

Let's further examine this "ambiguous middle" concept in Scripture. Remember, we were all born into Adam (Romans 5:12). We must all be born again into Christ. See if you can find an ambiguous middle in this broad biblical look at the redemption we have been given in Christ:

IN ADAM, YOU WERE:	IN CHRIST, YOU ARE:
Dark (Ephesians 5:8; John 3:19–20; Ephesians 4:18)	**Light** (Ephesians 5:8)
Goat (Matthew 25:32)	**Sheep** (Matthew 25:32; John 10:2–3)
Old (Romans 6:6)	**New** (2 Corinthians 5:17; Colossians 3:3; Romans 6:6; Galatians 2:20)
Sinner (Romans 5:8; James 5:20; Luke 15:7)	**Saint** (over 60 verses)
Unholy (1 Timothy 1:9)	**Holy** (Ephesians 1:4; Colossians 1:22)
Condemned (John 3:18)	**Blameless** (Ephesians 1:4; Colossians 1:22)

IN ADAM, YOU WERE:	IN CHRIST, YOU ARE:
In the domain of darkness (Colossians 1:13)	In the kingdom of light (Colossians 1:13)
A sinner, in darkness (Romans 5:8; Ephesians 4:18)	A saint in the light (Colossians 1:12)
Unrighteous (1 Corinthians 6:1, 9; 1 Peter 3:18)	Righteous (2 Corinthians 5:21)
Lost (Luke 15:4; 19:10)	Found (Luke 19:10; Matthew 18:11)
Impure (Galatians 5:19–21; Ephesians 4:18)	Pure (Titus 2:14)
Unregenerate (Ephesians 2:1; Titus 3:5)	Regenerated (Titus 3:5)
By nature a child of wrath (Ephesians 2:3)	A partaker of the divine nature (2 Peter 1:4)
Dead in sin (Ephesians 2:1; Romans 5:12)	Alive in Christ (Ephesians 2:5; Colossians 2:13; Romans 6:11)
In the flesh (Romans 7:5; Colossians 2:11)	In the Spirit (Romans 8:9; Galatians 5:24)
Rejected (Deuteronomy 32:20)	Reconciled (2 Corinthians 5:19; Romans 5:10)
Captive to sin (Titus 3:3; Romans 6:20)	Free from sin (Romans 6:7, 18, 22)
Perverted (Deuteronomy 32:20; Romans 7:14–24)	Perfected (Hebrews 10:14; Philippians 3:15)
Separated (Colossians 1:21; Ephesians 4:18)	Joined in one spirit to Jesus (1 Corinthians 6:17)

Wow! Let's take some time here. You might like to go through the above table prayerfully. Look up the verses mentioned and consider them in your heart. Are you pursuing freedom? Then do not brush over God's powerful declarations of that freedom listed above. We must take the truth to God in intimacy. We must dialogue with Him about how He sees us, crying out for understanding and for the reality of what He purchased us for. We must set our minds on these things so our lives can get in line with them (Romans 12:2; Colossians 3:2). That's how our experience conforms to the reality of our new nature.

As we can see in the above table, there is no ambiguous middle. Let it transition in your heart from information to revelation. The Greek word for "revelation" means "to make manifest."[1] It means you have tangible evidence of it, and you have *tasted and seen* it is true. Intimacy with God is the source of sustainable revelation. Give this the time it deserves to sink in deeply and nourish your inner man, whether you are new to this or you have read these verses a thousand times before. "Let the word of Christ dwell in you richly" (Colossians 3:16). You can outgrow *information*, but you can never outgrow *revelation*. It is alive; it never gets old or outdated. Never believe a lie that it does.

Scripture is not the source of our ambiguous middle ideology telling us we are somewhere between light and dark, both sinner and saint simultaneously. Scripture makes no allusion to an ambiguous middle. We must not either. The old in Adam *is gone.* The new in Christ *has come* (2 Corinthians 5:17). It is inescapably scriptural.

We have all had life experiences that make us feel as though we are somewhere in between Adam and Christ, as if we are a mixture of the old and new man. These can be familiar feelings or nagging memories of past sin and shame. When we let Scripture be our *only* reference for who we are, our experience looks more like the reality spoken of in this table.

Please do not misunderstand me here. The above statements are true about us, but *we* need to be diligent to grow in maturity and understanding. God has declared the truth, making it available in our experience, but He will not enforce it upon us at the cost of agreement from our human will. You will need to stand against the external temptations for sin and the fiery darts of the wicked one (that come from outside, not from within). You will need to gird up the loins of your mind in the truth and against deception (1 Peter 1:13). You must consider yourself dead to sin and alive to God in Christ (Romans 6:11). (We will look at simple, practical ways to do this later.)

I have felt waves of desire and challenges to my revelation that all Christians can feel, even since understanding and walking in this truth. This message helps me see them for what they really are, and I now stand a chance of living free and overcoming them. As I walk consistently in the truth, the intensity and volume of temptations fade, becoming dull, distant, and easier to distinguish and expose. Discipline, self-control, and maturity are still very much a new covenant responsibility though, even with a more accurate view of the dynamics of our salvation. I am now disciplining myself in the truth of who I already am, not to become it! This makes all the difference.

THE EAST FROM THE WEST

In case we have not discredited the ambiguous middle enough, let's look at a few more passages that give us no middle when identifying ourselves in Scripture.

> *"As far as the east is from the west, so far does he remove our transgressions from us."*
> **PSALMS 103:12**

The distance between the east and the west is eternal. The "old" man is not chasing you down, breathing down your neck, and resurrecting himself frequently to cause sin in your life. He is dead and gone (Romans 6:6; Galatians 2:20; Colossians 3:3). He was removed as far away as the east is from the west.

> *"I have blotted out your transgressions like a cloud and your sins like mist; return to me, for I have redeemed you."*
> **ISAIAH 44:22**

Despite the old covenant context of the above verse, it applies to us in a new covenant sense. Because of our experience struggling with sin, we believe our sinful nature is still very much alive. God declares He has blotted out our sin like mist. Redemption, in God's view, is not only an act on His behalf with eternal life in mind, but also a removal of the sinful nature itself, the thing that kept us in bondage. That is why one Greek word used for redemption is *lytroō*,[2] meaning "to deliver: from evils of every kind, internal and external."[3]

Now is probably a good time to mention the word "positional," a term that has done huge damage to our Christian experience. Positional is a word that acknowledges the Bible calls us something like "holy" or "light," but then explains why we do not have an experience of the Bible's statement. "It is positionally true, but not *tangibly* true" some might say—meaning it is real objectively but not subjectively. Or, it is real for our spirit man, but not our true self or "flesh man," or our soul (mind, will, and emotions). We are called to challenge our experience with the truth of Scripture so our lives can be transformed to live in real freedom. We are not called to make up terminology to stay in the same bondage or glaze over the promises of Scripture. There is nothing positional about the things we are looking at here, as we will continue to see.

> *"He has delivered us from the domain of darkness and*
> *transferred us to the kingdom of his beloved Son."*
> **COLOSSIANS 1:13**

Here you are in the kingdom of His beloved Son, or you are still in the domain of darkness. Again, no middle ground.

> *"For at one time you were darkness, but now you are light in*
> *the Lord. Walk as children of light."*
> **EPHESIANS 5:8**

There is not a "dim" option here, only dark or light. To make the statement about yourself that you are light with no darkness can be difficult—especially if you have concluded you are a mixture like "yin and yang" (a Chinese philosophy/New Age concept, not a scriptural one), part light and part dark. Agree with Scripture. You are light. The Bible tells you so.

We must not define ourselves by our lives or experiences, as though our experience is a better source of truth than the Scriptures.

The ambiguous middle idea has kept us in bondage. It has given us an excuse to live in persistent sin, confessing to ourselves we will never *really* be free from it, but thanking Him that His grace covers us in our sin anyway. Sinning may not remove His grace and mercy from us, but grace came to take sin *out* of us and empower freedom in our lives, not cover us *in* our sin. This small change of mind can manifest incredible freedom from sin in our lives, as well as consistent and unashamed intimacy with Father God.

You are finally compatible with God, adopted as a son or daughter in Christ, for the sake of knowing Him.

Let's agree that the old is gone. Not only that, let's agree the ambiguous middle is gone too. Both are equally as dangerous and harmful to our Christian lives. The ambiguous middle has been killing our hope, robbing our righteousness, and ruining our relationship with the Father. Enough is enough. No more middle.

Our problem is not that we still have a sinful nature. Our problem is we haven't realized we no longer have one!

(ENDNOTES)

1. Strong's G0602
2. Strong's G3084
3. W.E. Vine, M.A., *Vine's Complete Expository Dictionary of Old and New Testament Words* (Nashville: Thomas Nelson Inc., Indexed ed., 2003).

CHAPTER 3
BORN FROM ABOVE

Is it becoming clear now that the "sinner saved by grace" idea is not scriptural? Let's look at a few more concepts that contradict the paradigm. The term "born again" is one clear example of this. Every Christian knows of the term "born again," but do we really know what it means?[1]

I will never forget the night I was born again. I was nineteen years old. It was a traditional altar call in a Pentecostal church. Christine, my girlfriend at the time (now my wife), genuinely loved the Lord and longed for me to know God too, so we went to church together. I had "gone rogue." I had been raised in a beautiful Christian home, but I had run far away into the darkness of sin and death. The Holy Spirit simply and gently moved on my heart that night in such a way that I finally, personally, knew Jesus was real and He loved me. Christine had shown me such grace in our relationship that I was getting a strong idea of God's reality. Those two experiences combined were enough to cause me to respond and give my life to Him. It was not enough to know what it meant though.

Christine and I went out with my brother, Joe, and his wife, Katie, to celebrate my conversion, and we ate a huge platter of cheese at a dessert bar. I was more certain about the cheese than I was of my new identity, but I'd had an encounter with God and made a public decision to anchor myself in moving forward. A few challenging years followed as I grappled with a strong desire to know God, but an even greater sense of incompatibility kept me from Him. In hindsight, I would not change a thing about my journey in understanding, no matter how dynamic, emotional, and up and down it has been. God would not rob me of the adventure of coming to know Him by my will, and He would use all the ways I missed His heart along the way to bring clarity and health to others.

I can relate to many of the different theological persuasions and personal challenges people face as we learn to relate to God and find true freedom. I went from Arminianism to Calvinism to multiple other "isms," and then back again. I went in theological circles, subtly trying to fulfill my desire for the person of God with theological positions instead. I went from seven days a week of church services to a season of being angry at the church and sulking at home. I tried home churches, café churches, small churches, big churches, and the lot. I got hung up on social justice expressions of church (talking about it, at least). I got hung up on the general *method* of the church, without realizing it was the simple, tangible *message* of the cross I needed to grasp. I deeply love the bride these days, after finally meeting the Bridegroom and seeing how He loves His girl, in all her shapes and sizes.

I moved into a self-produced holiness theology, becoming arrogant and judgmental with every new measure of purity I could muster up without God's help. When I became exhausted from working up my holiness, I discovered a perverted grace mindset, gathered teachers to suit my passions and lick my wounds of offense, and indulged in sin with a huge misunderstanding of His grace. I have had an extensive preview of how the things we believe determine our behaviors, and how devastating it is to be wrong about the truth. I eventually pursued the miraculous, before accurately identifying myself in Christ alone, making signs and wonders a source of introspection and measurement for my acceptance in God instead of an exciting pursuit of glorifying His name. Having come out the other side of such experiences, I am eager to save many some trouble. The less time we take figuring out the simple truth of Christ and Him crucified, and the plain reality of our salvation, the more time we can spend living whole lives, knowing God, and reaching the great harvest with pure motives.

The Greek term for born again, *gennao anothen,* actually means "born from above."[2] It also means to be born anew, or to be born "from the beginning, from the very first." What was Adam like in the beginning? He was created in the image and likeness of God (Genesis 1:26–27). To be born again means to be born from the beginning, or born from above, which refers to heaven. That is why "our citizenship is in heaven" (Philippians 3:20) and we are seated "in the heavenly places in Christ" (Ephesians 2:6). Heaven is not only our new home, it is now our origin too! The purity of Adam's nature before the fall is now our nature in union with Christ.

> *We are not born again in our sin;*
> *we are born again from our sin.*

Even the Greek word for "reconciled" means "to change from one condition to another, so as to remove all enmity and leave no impediment to unity and peace!"[3] We have been restored to a state of "former harmony" by the removal of the sinful nature that kept us at odds with God (2 Corinthians 5:18–19; Romans 5:10; Colossians 1:20). Nothing about this is a future promise. It is a present tense existence in Christ. Now that is good news!

"Born again" doesn't mean nothing about us really changes, but one day we can go to heaven. There is nowhere in Scripture that alludes to this limited view of our rebirth. It means a new existence right now.

"As you sent me into the world,
so I have sent them into the world."
JOHN 17:18

How can Jesus send us into the world in the same way He was sent into the world by the Father? He was sent from heaven to earth. Why would Jesus say something like this (also John 20:21)? If we are born from above now, then we are also sent from heaven to earth! That is why we are "not of this world" (John 17:16). Remember, these Scriptures are not poetic catchphrases Jesus or the apostles came up with to tickle our ears. They are the truth, declared by Almighty God in Scripture, which "cannot be broken" (John 10:35).

COMING OUT OF THE BAPTISM TANK

If we believe we are sinners saved by grace, it is like we have gone halfway through the baptism process. Imagine that you show up for your baptism ceremony, excited to perform an "outward expression of the inward reality" you believe you have. You mount the platform in front of the church, make statements about your faith, and then the minister dunks you. Instead of a brief submersion, though, you are held under the water until the bubbles stop! You then remain in the tank for good, while they move on to the next person in line. First, if this really happened, there would be serious court cases being held against the church. Second, sadly this would be a more accurate outward expression of what many of us believe is true.

*"Having been buried with him in baptism, in which you were
also raised with him through faith in the powerful working of
God, who raised him from the dead."*
COLOSSIANS 2:12

Baptism represents the reality that we have died with Christ *and* have been raised in His likeness with the newness of life (also Romans 6:4). It is an outward expression of an inward reality. It is not an expression of a positional reality, but a real one. Baptism is not a ritualistic next step in our faith. It is not an obligatory event to show others we are serious about Jesus. The statement you make when you go under the water in baptism is that His death was actually your death. When you reemerge from the water, you declare you have been raised with Him in His likeness and His resurrection, and you reflect a new life.

Too many of us believe we are *covered* in our sin and kept in a standby state, not subject to wrath anymore but also not redeemed. It is the ambiguous middle all over again. We believe we were baptized into a future hope rather than death to sin with Christ.

This is like going down under the water, representing your future death, but instead of coming up and living the newness of life in Christ, you stay dead in your sin, uncomfortably holding your breath and awaiting your future resurrection.

We were converted by the cross, not covered by it.

Jesus only gave us two physical sacraments to do in the new covenant: baptism and communion (Luke 22:19; Matthew 26:26–29; 28:19). He is not interested in meaningless rituals, and He was not looking to get a kick out of seeing us in our frumpy baptism gowns. When you consider these two things and what they mean, you find they explicitly represent

Jesus's death and resurrection and our personal union with that death and resurrection.

The Greek word used to describe communion or the Lord's Supper is *koinōnia*, which is the same word translated "fellowship." This means "joint participation." It is an intimate and personal word.[4] We were intimately joined to Christ in His death and resurrection. Communion is a constant celebration and reminder of this.

> *"The cup of blessing that we bless, is it not a participation (koinōnia) in the blood of Christ? The bread that we break, is it not a participation (koinōnia) in the body of Christ?"*
> **1 CORINTHIANS 10:16**

We must not take the bread and wine if we don't believe we have been set free from sin through co-crucifixion and co-resurrection in Christ. We also should not water baptize new believers until they have understood what it represents: a death to the old, sinful nature and a new life in Christ as saints. Does this seem too narrow-minded? Well, who decided that "narrow" was a negative attitude rather than a liberating one? It is time we got narrow about the truth that leads to abundant life.

If you have already been water baptized without this revelation, do not feel condemned. Your internal reality of new life exists regardless of your motives for being baptized. Renew your value and revelation of baptism now and live in the fullness of what yours really represented. I was baptized to get my pastor's and parents' approval as a teenager. I deeply undervalued baptism and communion. These days they are our Darwin church community's most valued practices. We break bread nearly every time we meet, and we celebrate new life by baptizing people. It is our core message as a community. It is the most incredible representation of our new existence in Christ. It does not cause our new life to manifest, but it certainly represents it and makes it more tangible for each person embracing the truth about his or her new life.

THE NEVER-ENDING CIRCUMCISION

Another powerful way our conversion is represented in Scripture is by circumcision. For Jews, circumcision is highly valued as a practice. Even during World War II, at a time when someone discovered to be circumcised was often killed, Jewish boys would still be circumcised on the eighth day. They would even perform circumcision in secret within Nazi labor camps.[5] Circumcision is a remarkable sign of the covenant God made with Abraham (Genesis 12:1–3; 15:18–21; 17:10–12) and that Jesus eventually fulfilled.

> *"And if you are Christ's, then you are Abraham's offspring, heirs according to promise."*
> **GALATIANS 3:29**

As in much of the old covenant, there are physical shadows for us of a spiritual reality that we have in the new covenant. We are not the physical offspring of Abraham, but we are his spiritual offspring as those who have inherited the promises made to his descendants by God. These promises are fulfilled in the new covenant. In the same way, people of old underwent a physical circumcision; we also must undergo a true spiritual circumcision to be a part of the new covenant in Christ.

> *"In him also you were circumcised with a circumcision made without hands, by putting off the body of the flesh, by the circumcision of Christ,"*
> **COLOSSIANS 2:11**

Paul describes our circumcision in Christ as a "putting off the body of the flesh." The flesh here represents the sinful nature we have been set free from and paints a picture of us having had it circumcised off us. He refers to us in our old life as having been "dead in our trespasses and the uncircumcision of our flesh" (Colossians 2:13). Our nature in Adam was uncircumcision; our nature in Christ is circumcision. So what gets removed (circumcised) from us at conversion? The "old" man, the sinful nature we inherited in Adam. In the old covenant, circumcision was a removal of the foreskin of the male as a sign of the promises God made to Abraham. Likewise, in the new covenant, the foreskin that is removed is the sinful nature, as a sign of the promises now received in Christ!

How long does it take to get circumcised? Is it a lifelong process? No. We have made it one if we believe we are slowly dying to the old man or the sinful nature. Circumcision is best when it is as swift as possible. Additionally, if the old man or sinful nature in this shadow of circumcision represents the foreskin, then what are we doing carrying that thing around with us now that it is cut off? That would be weird. It is removed, useless, and needs to be discarded.

Remember, there is no middle ground in the gospel. You are uncircumcised or circumcised. If a doctor did half a job of it, you could probably sue him for half his wealth. Jesus is the doctor in this analogy, and He does not do half a job of your circumcision. He also does not ask you to do it yourself. He did it for you.

Your new life is not just another go at the old Adamic life. It is not a slow renovation of the sin-stained home that was your existence. God does not make something beautiful of your broken life, no matter how nice this sentiment seems. Instead, He gives you a new life in Christ. It is a total demolition of the old, sinful nature in Christ and a new house of holiness He built when you believed. He thinks it is a house suitable for a king, by the way; that is why He lives in you now.

We must not believe a philosophy of the Christian life that represents a lifelong circumcision, or a half-done baptism. These faulty ways of thinking lead to faulty ways of living.

(ENDNOTES)

1. See John 3 for where Jesus speaks about what it is to be born again or "born from above."
2. Strong's G0509
3. Blue Letter Bible. "Reconcile, Reconciliation." www.blueletterbible.org/search/dictionary/viewTopic.cfm?topic=VT0002324.
4. Strong's G2842
5. The Central Council of Jews in Germany. "Why do Jews circumcise their children?" www.zentralratderjudenindeutschland.de/down/Dossier-Beschneidungen.pdf.

CHAPTER 4
AWAKE, O SLEEPER

"For anything that becomes visible is light. Therefore it says, 'Awake, O sleeper, and arise from the dead, and Christ will shine on you.'"
EPHESIANS 5:14

One exciting thing about the righteousness message is the language defining it: It is to "awake" (1 Corinthians 15:34; Ephesians 5:14). We don't have to spend years figuring out the nuts and bolts of the message before we can experience the liberation of it. There is a simple heart stirring and liberation experience that happens in a moment as we finally understand that our salvation means far more than we thought. The quality of this liberty increases as we grow in intimacy with God and understanding, learning to meditate on the truth, fighting for it, even as opposing thoughts and feelings may come.

Where the enemy has kept us in experiential bondage by causing us to believe we *are* what we *are not*, the truth can liberate us dramatically and swiftly from these lies. Time and time again, I have watched people realize the things they have been battling for years have already been defeated in Christ. There has been instant freedom on so many occasions—even without ongoing counseling or constant ministry. I could share many testimonies of people being set free from many lies, and the diverse symptoms of these lies, that rise to challenge the far-reaching freedom reality the blood of Christ enables us to have. Decades of PTSD (post-traumatic stress disorder), medicated depression, drug-induced psychosis, anxiety, panic, fear, and many psychological issues are broken by the truth as it is elevated along with faith—not to mention the thousands of healing miracles that take place when the finished work of Jesus is exalted, and Holy Spirit honored.

I realize some who read this may experience some of these things. We live in what secular sociologists have called an "age of anxiety." Mental disorders are not the Christian inheritance Jesus paid for, and the church *can* look different to the world. It can take courage and some investment in the truth, but the blood of Jesus is that powerful. I promise you I can relate to those who are experiencing these things. Telling you freedom is easier than you thought it was is not being insensitive to the tangible reality of the issues. Let me share my story with you.

MY PERSONAL AWAKENING

Besides being addicted to pornography for years, riddled with self-consciousness and selfishness, and not knowing who I was, for a time I also suffered all manners of psychological attacks. I was traveling in India with friends once when I accidentally took a heavy hallucinogenic drug that did serious damage to my mind, resulting in a significant demonic attack against my soul. For nine hours I was tormented by demonic visions and voices. I was a Christian, in my mid-twenties, in the "perverted grace" season of my Christian walk I mentioned earlier. I had believed in Jesus at the age of nineteen but had never learned who I was, nor of the power and authority I had as a son. I was living in ignorance, frustration, and sin. My Christian experience was one of unfulfilled desire. I was desperate to know God but trapped behind a thick veil of perceived incompatibility with Him. Being kept from the comfort of compatible intimacy with God because of lack of understanding, I tried to find comfort in sin instead—selfishness, drinking, lust, and arrogance. I had become incompatible with sin as a Christian though, so was more miserable than ever.

For the next four months after taking the drug, I heard voices speaking of suicide, compelling me to be silent or I might die in some freak accident. I felt as though I was still lost in that drug-induced state. The voices tormented me. They told me constant lies about my worth and God. They declared doom over my marriage, family, and life. I had crippling panic attacks which became so bad that I physically could not move, sometimes for hours. I would lie on a bed crushed by the overwhelming feelings, heart racing, sweating, and losing my mind. I was claustrophobic to where I could not drive my car without the windows down. I couldn't deal with tunnels or planes either. I felt so fragile, like I was an empty soft drink can, rolling around the dance floor at a vigorous bush dance.[1] Things were bad. I was breaking inside and felt trapped in my mind. These constant attacks lasted over four months. I cannot truly put words to the torment I went through. Impending doom is not an overstatement of how I felt. When this started for me in India, my wife was suddenly attacked by similar symptoms all the way back in Australia. She had to move back in with her parents until I returned home. She had not even taken drugs like I had. These concurrent episodes helped us recognize the demonic dynamic to our experience, but we were stuck about how to be free from it.

In the middle of a crippling panic attack one day, months into this ordeal, I found the courage, despite the voices bullying me into silence, to call my brother, Timothy. He is a man who knows who he is and can believe it for others too, even when they do not see it. As I sobbed over the phone, telling Tim the things I was going through, his response was to quiet me down finally and speak to me immediately of the answer, rather than reveling in the problem with me.

He said something like, "I am going to pray some things about who you really are over you. When I do, those things you have been tormented by will leave." It sounded insane to me in my deception. How could it be so simple? Wouldn't I need years of counseling for this mess? But I agreed, my situation having robbed me of the liberty to be proud.

He prayed over me the same things I have been speaking about so far in this book, that:

- I am seated in heavenly places in Christ,
- I am accepted in the beloved,
- I am light with no darkness,
- I am delivered from the enemy's grasp,
- and so on.

Because he believed these things were still the absolute subjective truth about me as a son of God, the presence of God immediately filled the room I was in. Where God had felt so distant just a moment earlier, He was now very evident in my situation. I felt the jealousy of God toward me. I felt His violent love and desire for my freedom, as though what was happening to me was utterly illegal. The feelings, thoughts, and voices instantly vanished! The anxiety, fear, and paranoia left. I was free! My wife walked boldly into freedom as well during this time, as we grew in understanding.

I wrote this book on a small indigenous island off the east coast of the Northern Territory—Groote Eylandt. We lived in a tiny community of only one thousand people. My wife is a medical doctor and was completing a six-month, rural, medical placement there. The only way on and off the island is a rather small airplane, and it is very isolated there. I still never feel fear, anxiety, or panic. I never feel claustrophobic. I am a confident son, found in the faithfulness of a very good Father. Years later, and for the rest of my life, I am still free. Regardless of what life may present, the truth will never change. It is absolute. It is a person. It is Jesus. I promise my circumstances have not been smooth sailing, not by any stretch. In fact, currently, Christine and I are in some of the most challenging circumstances we have ever faced. But there is an anchor of truth now that will never be moved, despite what may come. When we fight to stay established in Him, the freedom and peace the truth produces can become as unchanging as the truth itself.

I have learned (the hard way) that when we do not know who we are, the enemy will do his best to keep it that way. He will then take advantage of our ignorance and lead us into more death, loss, and destruction (John 10:10). While I experienced an amazing freedom that day when my brother prayed for me, I somehow recognized it would not keep me free. The Bible says we will "*know the truth* and the truth will set you free" (John 8:32, emphasis mine). It does not say you will know an experience of freedom and the experience of freedom will keep you free.

To have a tangible experience when someone believes the truth *for you* in a situation is powerful, liberating, and life changing. But maintaining a transformed and liberated life happens when you pursue that *understanding of the truth for yourself.* I delved deeply into Scripture to discover my identity in Christ and grow in relationship with the Father. When a strong feeling of anxiety knocked at the door of my soul some months later, I was not caught off guard. I had built my understanding in a place of intimacy and was unwilling to be convinced otherwise. The goodness of God and the truth of my redemption had become far too real to me to give in to this lie. I had built my house on the rock of truth while there was no storm, *acting* on the things I found about myself. When the storm brewed, I could confront it with truth and watch the storm vanish.

Because of my pursuit of truth, I did not have to use the *experience* of freedom from previous months to combat an *experience* of bondage I was now encountering. I fought the suggestion to give myself to anxiety again with the *truth*. After a couple of moments of that same familiar feeling of fear, heart rate increasing, becoming dizzy, and thoughts flying through my head questioning my freedom in Christ, I sat up and talked to the Father. I thanked Him for the incredible freedom He had given me in Christ. I thanked Him that in Christ, I was actually free from anxiety. As I dwelled on the truth in a place of intimacy, it took only moments for the feeling to be exposed for its powerlessness and to flee the room!

> *Instead of letting what I was feeling change my mind about the truth, I turned to the truth to challenge what I was feeling.*

That is how the gospel works. The same goes with lust, fear, anger, self-consciousness, body image issues, anxiety, and more. We must fight to believe what the Bible says is true. These things have been removed from our lives in Christ. Any experience of them is an outside suggestion from the enemy, and from the "broadcast of sin" still on the earth. We have the power to never identify ourselves with them, being strong in the truth. (We will look more practically at this later in the book.) I pray in faith that many who read my testimony, who are dealing with similar things, will experience the same manifest reality of freedom. The truth is that powerful. The blood of Jesus is that strong. I declare rampant freedom from these issues over every reader dealing with lies.

I will never stop proclaiming the truth of our tangible and inherited identity in Christ. Without it, my life would honestly be a write-off.

My experience of freedom is lasting because I have pursued truth and intimacy. It is not an exception to the normal Christian experience. It is one example of thousands as this awakening to righteousness shakes hearts and lives all over the world. If this was just a fancy new theological language to associate with or to build a community around, but then live as we did before, I would be wasting my time and would not bother. However, freedom looks like something and Jesus paid for us to have it. I desire to see manifest freedom and powerful intimacy with God cover the earth. I have not lived perfectly since my experience of freedom and growth in the truth. At times, I have had to fight to remind myself of the truth, but nonetheless, I live a life now of purity, freedom, and clarity of conscience I never thought possible.

It is time for an overhaul. My desire is that in my lifetime, I will see the "sinner saved by grace" oxymoron completely eradicated from the global Christian church. It is not just a difference of opinion. It is not an alternative biblical possibility. It is 100 percent non-scriptural and extremely destructive. Why am I so passionate about this? Is it because I am distracted and defined by a precious intellectual theology? No. It is because there is a real war going on. Lives hang in the balance. The liberty of the human soul is at stake. The quality of our blood-bought freedom is under threat. For too long we have worn shackles of sin, shame, bondage, and confusion.

The way we have identified ourselves in the church, by the very thing Jesus paid to make us free from, must be exposed. We must repent. We must move forward in the truth. There is a harvest of souls to be won for the kingdom of light, a devil trying to stop it, and millions of powerful people in the church fully able to establish the kingdom of God on the earth. We must recognize the identity, inheritance, and intimacy with God that is ours. We must behave like the bride we really are, destroying the works of darkness and knowing the Father in purity and truth.

Decide today. Put off the "sinner saved by grace" idea once and for all. Become "dead to sinner." Choose with me that our generation will see the truth of salvation invade every corner of the earth. We will be righteous radicals in word and deed. We will be fundamentally *known for knowing Him*. We will be known for the power and love that result from the true intimacy with God that Jesus's precious blood was shed for us to enjoy.

(ENDNOTES)

1. Bush dance is a style of dance from Australia, particularly where the music is provided by a bushband. The dances are mainly based on the traditional folk dances of the UK, Ireland and central Europe.

PART TWO

THE RIGHTEOUSNESS OF GOD IN CHRIST

CHAPTER 5

WHAT IS RIGHTEOUSNESS?

"May we not deceive ourselves, imagining that sinning is inevitable for a Christian, I think no thought hurts our Lord more than this kind of attitude."

WATCHMAN NEE[1]

As the "sinner saved by grace" misdiagnosis rapidly diminishes, we need to define ourselves as Christians. This way we can better understand and live the intended Christian life: a life of intimacy, power, and love. A biblical definition for Christians is that we are righteous,[2] as righteous as God, in fact. This is because in Christ we *become* God's righteousness, for the sake of a compatible relationship with Him and for the freedom He desires for us. Let's examine this.

"For our sake he made him to be sin who knew no sin, so that in him we might become the righteousness of God."
2 CORINTHIANS 5:21

In Scripture, a standard for righteousness is determined by the object it is being compared to. Righteousness according to the old covenant law, for example, would be someone living up to the law perfectly (Philippians 3:6; Luke 1:6; Romans 10:5). To break even one law would make someone unrighteous according to the law (James 2:10). It is all or nothing. To live up to the law would make you righteous according to that standard, or "right" regarding all the law demands. Similarly, a righteous or just scale is one that weighs accurately (Job 31:6; Proverbs 16:11). It measures up to its intended design. Righteousness, when God Himself is the object it is defined by, is to be just like Him. He is the standard. He defines what righteousness is. Righteousness does not define what He is. When compared with God's righteousness, everything else is essentially unrighteousness. The only way for us to be compatible with God and righteous before Him is to share His righteousness. We could never produce our own of such quality.

As sinners under the law, the Israelites tried to produce righteousness in their own strength, according to the law's standard (Romans 10:3). The sinful nature made this a very difficult task, as the purpose of the law proved, provoking them to sin all the more (Romans 5:20; Galatians 2:16, 3:21–25). Hence the sacrificial system: to cover their sins while they awaited a better covenant, which would enable tangible freedom from the fallen human condition (Hebrews 8:6). The sinful nature was their true problem, which the law continually reminded them of (Romans 7:7–12; Hebrews 10:1–4). They could not live up to the righteousness the old covenant law demanded, let alone the very nature of God the new covenant demands. In the new covenant, the righteousness of God is also *provided* by God—in Christ, through faith, which is the powerful difference between the old and new covenants. The sinful nature is removed in Christ (Romans 6:6; Galatians 2:20; Colossians 2:11–15; 3:3) and we receive His nature. We do not earn this transformation of ourselves, by our efforts, or because we deserve it. There is nothing we can do to attain God's righteousness—it is given by the grace, purpose, and pleasure of God as soon as we individually believe in Christ for salvation.

"For as by the one man's disobedience the many were made sinners, so by the one man's obedience the many will be made righteous."
ROMANS 5:19

See the exchange that takes place here (also 2 Corinthians 5:21) of our sinfulness for His righteousness? In Adam, we inherited a sinful nature. This was not a positionally sinful nature, but a real one. Sin stained us in our entire being. In Christ, we inherit God's righteous nature, not positionally, but actually. This also affects our entire being. This becomes *experiential* in our lives as we engage in intimacy with God, understanding, and faithful obedience to the truth. Our independent will must engage with the truth for it to manifest and become our experience.

Scripture uses the term "righteous" to describe the resulting state of our regeneration and our compatibility with God: our likeness to Him. It means we have "right-standing" with God, or more simply, God's "rightness" has been given to us. As partakers of the divine nature (2 Peter 1:3; 1 John 4:17), through regeneration by Holy Spirit (Titus 3:5), God's divine righteousness is imputed and imparted to us in Christ (2 Corinthians 5:17, 21; Romans 1:16–17, 3:21; Philippians 3:9; 1 Peter 2:24). When we are born again, it completely replaces the old, sinful nature inside us. This makes us right with God. This is what it means to be born of God (John 1:12–13). Because of this righteousness the Father has shared with us, we can accurately be called saints, holy, pure, blameless, and light-filled in Christ.

The reality that we share God's righteousness means many powerful things for us, including:

- We have an entirely new existence. We are those who are righteous before God in Christ, having peace with God, as if we had never sinned.

- Sharing God's righteousness makes us compatible with God so that we can have a deep, constant, love relationship with the Father.

- Due to our righteous nature in Christ and because of our new relationship quality with the Father, we can now live a righteous life as a love response to Him—the thing we could never do with our old, sinful nature and broken relationship.

To further understand how significant this is, let's look at the difference between imputed righteousness and imparted righteousness.

IMPUTED RIGHTEOUSNESS:

Your name is written in heaven right now (Luke 10:20; Philippians 4:3; Hebrews 12:23) because of the blood of Jesus (Revelation 21:27), shed for your salvation. Your name is written in the Book of Life, where the *righteous* are enrolled (Psalms 69:28), because that is what your salvation purchased for you. This means you have legal liberation from your previously sinful life. You are justified (considered as though you have never sinned) by faith (Romans 5:1). You are forgiven by the blood of Jesus (Ephesians 1:7). His perfect life lived has been transferred to your spiritual "account." God will not see you in any other way but through the perfect life of His Son. This is essentially what imputed righteousness is. He *sees you* as righteous. Even if you still had a sinful nature, He would see you according to His Son's life. Through faith, you have Jesus's indestructible record of holiness qualifying you for eternal life. This is a deeply profound, merciful, and gracious act of God for us, which cannot be devalued.

IMPARTED RIGHTEOUSNESS

In the same way that the sunlight cannot be separated from the sun, *imputed* righteousness can never be separated from *imparted* righteousness. To stop at imputed righteousness would leave us believing we remain evil but we get a "Jesus suit" to wear, hiding our sinful state underneath. When the Father looks at us, He doesn't see Jesus *instead* of us. A sheet of "Jesus glass" doesn't stand between the Father and us, concealing our sin from Him when He views us through it. Sadly, many Christians believe this is the case. This idea leaves us incompatible with Him, but because of the supposed veil over His eyes, hiding our sin from Him, we are able to relate to Him. If this were true, it would mean Jesus's real purpose behind the atonement on the cross was to play a trick on the Father— to pull sheep wool over His eyes to disguise the goats standing before Him—rather than Jesus coming to partner with the everlasting Father of love, in the power of Holy Spirit, to destroy sin and death, converting us back to righteousness and relationship with God. Without imparted righteousness, God is made out to be foolish and the Son deceitful toward Him, claiming we are something we are not.

He sees us righteous because He made us righteous.

God imparts His righteousness to you in the regeneration of Holy Spirit so you can know Him intimately. The blood of Jesus paid for imparted righteousness as much as it did imputed righteousness. It is His blood that washed you and made you righteous (Revelation 1:5). This means when the Father looks at you, He actually sees *you*. He loves what He sees too! This opens you to an accessible relationship with Him. Jesus came for righteousness's sake. You have become righteous in Christ, not forensically, or positionally, but actually.

The simple recovery of biblical truth that people all over the planet are awakening to is this:

Righteousness is not only an imputed position that God declares toward us. It is also an imparted reality in our nature right now because of our union with Him in Christ, removing the sinful nature, and making manifest holiness and pure relationship available to us.

It is not imbalanced to say righteousness *is* the message of the gospel. The righteousness of God, which we share with Him in Christ, sets us free from the old man and makes intimacy with God available again. The writer of Hebrews referred to the message of Christ as the "word of *righteousness*" (Hebrews 5:13). Paul explained that the Scriptures are for training and teaching us in *righteousness* (2 Timothy 3:15–16). The old covenant *pointed* us toward *righteousness*, while the new covenant *provided* it for us (Romans 3:21–31). The gospel is the power of God unto salvation because the *righteousness* of God is revealed in it (Romans 1:17). Peter said Jesus "bore our sins in His body on the tree, so that we might die to sin and live to *righteousness*" (1 Peter 2:24). This means God's righteousness, in exchange for our sin, is the central theme of the atonement itself. Jesus is called the sun of *righteousness* (Malachi 4:2), rising for us with healing for our sinful condition. He is also called Jesus Christ the *righteous* (1 John 2:1), modeling in His earthly life the substance of what a righteous life unlocks for us. Jesus came to preach *righteousness* as the means by which He brings us back to the Father (John 14:6). "Having been set free from sin, you became slaves of *righteousness*" (Romans 6:18). Our new life in Christ, after the sin issue is removed, is one of slavery to the righteousness of God. We are commanded to "seek first the kingdom of God and *his righteousness*" (Matthew 6:33). The old covenant was labeled "the ministry of condemnation," while the new covenant was called "the ministry of *righteousness*" (2 Corinthians 3:9). Here is a prophetic statement from Jesus in the Psalms, declaring the message He came to declare:

"I have proclaimed the good news of righteousness in the great assembly; indeed, I do not restrain my lips, O Lord, You Yourself know. I have not hidden Your righteousness within my heart; I have declared Your faithfulness and Your salvation; I have not concealed Your lovingkindness and Your truth from the great assembly."
PSALMS 40:9–10 NKJV

As you can see, righteousness is the substance of our salvation. It results from our union with the death and resurrection of Christ. God's righteousness has been shared with us. This is why He can rightly call us sons and daughters. It is the reason the New Testament Epistles refer to us as saints (over sixty times) and not sinners. Because we are righteous now in Him, Holy Spirit has pleasure and compatibility in occupying us without being unequally yoked to unrighteousness (2 Corinthians 6:14–18). That righteousness is an imparted reality, not only an imputed declaration, and is transforming multitudes—when they honor and walk in this truth into supernatural intimacy with God and righteous, holy living.

A GREEK DEFINITION FOR A HEBREW CONCEPT

There are multiple Hebrew words for righteousness in the Old Testament.[3] There are also multiple Greek words for it in the New Testament.[4] The prominent theme in various Old Testament Hebrew words is an *imputed* righteousness rather than an *imparted* one. Abram is the clearest recipient of this imputed righteousness (Genesis 15:6).

The Hebrew word used for the righteousness imputed to Abram is ṣeḏâqâ.[5] It indicates a position given by God in light of Abram's faith. It means God considered Abram as righteous, despite Abram's sinful nature or his ability to keep any law—a huge act of mercy from God. Abram reached through the veil of time, benefiting in part from the sacrifice of the Lamb slain before the foundation of the world (Revelation 13:8;

1 Peter 1:20). He was counted righteous for his faith in God; however, there is no evidence *regeneration* happened, or the actual nature of those in the old covenant was made righteous. This was imputed righteousness, as we defined above.

This is the type of righteousness many Christians believe they have in the new covenant. However, in the new covenant, the apostles interpreted the reality of righteousness further, giving new covenant substance to an old covenant shadow.

When regeneration in Christ became a chronological possibility in history, righteousness had to be newly understood. A Greek word translated "justification" is *dikaiōsis* in the New Testament (e.g. Romans 4:25). This word means the same imputed righteousness as the Hebrew words used in the Old Testament. In fact, the concept is contrasted directly back to the imputed justification Abraham received in Romans 4. However, the Greek words used for righteousness in the New Testament differ from this word for justification and expand on it, showing imputed righteousness is not the end of our redemption but the beginning. These new definitions used to describe new covenant righteousness drastically moved from that of imputation to become definitions that now included imparted righteousness.

> *We have an actual righteous nature now in Christ, meaning we can live actual righteous lives by faith.*

We see words for "righteous" like *dikaios*.[6] When you look at this word in *Strong's Concordance*, it means: "used of him whose way of thinking, feeling, and acting is wholly conformed to the will of God, and who therefore needs no rectification in the heart or life;" also "faultless, guiltless," "holy and innocent," "acceptable to God." (Matthew 13:49; Romans 1:17; Galatians 3:11; Hebrews 10:38; 1 Peter 4:18). This is both a statement of our new nature and the life we are invited to live by faith as new creations. This is an internal reality being described, not just how God sees us.

Another word for righteousness is *dikaiosynē*,[7] which means the "state of him who is as he ought to be, righteousness, the *condition* acceptable to God, the doctrine concerning how man may attain *a state* approved of God," and "integrity, virtue, purity of life, rightness; correctness of thinking, feeling, and acting."[8] This word expands on the word for justification again, giving it a far deeper new covenant meaning now that we are united in Christ and one spirit with the Lord (1 Corinthians 6:17). This shows that our actual *condition* and *state* before God is one of righteousness, not just our position. We also see that as we continue faithfully in this truth, this naturally leads to purity of action too.

Then there is *dikaioo*,[9] meaning "to render (i.e. show) just or innocent: free, justify, be righteous. To render righteous or such he ought to be, to show, exhibit, evince, one to be righteous, such as he is and wishes himself to be considered" (Romans 3:24; 8:30; 1 Corinthians 6:11; Galatians 2:16; Titus 3:7).

You can see that while the definition of these Greek words includes our justified position before the Father, they go far deeper and reveal the statement of our new identity and ability to evidence our new nature in this life.

> *God's righteousness is far more than a positional intangibility to us. It is the reality of our regenerated state as Christians.*

We have already seen in part 1 how the old, sinful nature was crucified with Christ. The following verses further show that once you die and are raised with Christ in the new covenant, you share God's righteousness in your new nature:

"For our sake he made him to be sin who knew no sin, so that in him we might become the righteousness of God."
2 CORINTHIANS 5:21

"Not having a righteousness of my own that comes from the law, but that which comes through faith in Christ, the righteousness from God that depends on faith."
PHILIPPIANS 3:9

"For I am not ashamed of the gospel, for it is the power of God for salvation to everyone who believes, to the Jew first and also to the Greek. For in it the righteousness of God is revealed from faith for faith, as it is written, 'The righteous shall live by faith.'"
ROMANS 1:16-17

"And because of him you are in Christ Jesus, who became to us wisdom from God, righteousness and sanctification and redemption."
1 CORINTHIANS 1:30

"But now the righteousness of God has been manifested apart from the law, although the Law and the Prophets bear witness to it— the righteousness of God through faith in Jesus Christ for all who believe. For there is no distinction: for all have sinned and fall short of the glory of God, and are justified by his grace as a gift, through the redemption that is in Christ Jesus."
ROMANS 3:21-24

"For, being ignorant of the righteousness of God, and seeking to establish their own, they did not submit to God's righteousness. For Christ is the end of the law for righteousness to everyone who believes."
ROMANS 10:3-4

THE "DOING" OF RIGHTEOUSNESS

As you can see, righteousness is the powerful definition of your new identity. It is also the practical calling of your new life in Christ:

> *"Little children, let no one deceive you. Whoever practices righteousness is righteous, as he is righteous."*
> **1 JOHN 3:7**

We must not fall into the dangerous idea we can define ourselves by something without expecting and pursuing the manifest reality of that identity. The apostle John was confronted with an issue of people who practiced sin but paraded themselves as righteous in their language alone. He made the sobering statement that without actively living out righteousness by faith; we contradict the message. Our imparted righteousness functions from the relationship, faith, and understanding of what we have become, rather than trying to become something by reaching a given standard. But our imparted righteousness should function nonetheless.

Righteousness is what God *does* because righteous is what God *is* (Exodus 9:27; Ezra 9:15; Psalms 11:7; 119:137; John 17:25; Acts 3:13; 2 Corinthians 5:21). The reason God works perfect justice and righteousness in His actions is because He is righteous in His nature and character. His actions are an expression of His nature. When He behaves in holiness, He is Himself. This is the same nature which we are transformed into the moment we are born again. Therefore, when we clearly see who we are and walk in this truth obediently and faithfully, righteousness becomes what we do, because righteous is what we are.

Do you remember Will the eagle (who once was a chicken)? Consider that even though Will became an eagle in an instant, it was still his personal responsibility to define himself by this truth, and to spread those wings and fly out of the coop! He had to put some faith in the capabilities of his new eagle wings and get them moving. He had to take off from the ground despite that accustomed identity and familiarity of the chicken life. He had to trust that the chicken was dead. The other eagle could help him see the truth, but he could not flap Will's wings and fly into freedom for him.

> *We cannot practice righteousness until we believe*
> *we have become righteous.*

While it requires intentionality and diligence in the truth, we are now empowered to live practical, righteous lives without striving, because God recreated us as naturally righteous people who share His righteousness. In the past, we have seen ourselves as sinners but strived to live holy lives because we knew we should. Now, we get to see ourselves as we really are and learn to *act natural,* to spread our wings and fly. We must set our minds on things above (Colossians 3:2), allowing the experiential reality of our new life to invade our existence as we learn to walk with God. Our righteous behavior will not save us, our faith in Jesus saves us. Our righteous behavior is our honor, privilege, and purpose as we imitate our Father as His beloved children (Ephesians 5:1). The old mantra "Be yourself" is more relevant to the church than ever!

> *Righteousness is a **being** word before it is a **doing** word,*
> *but it is explicitly both.*

We must get this identity established in our hearts before expecting to live righteous lives. Jesus said, "Seek first the kingdom of God *and his righteousness*" (Matthew 6:33), indicating that without discovering and sharing God's righteousness by faith in Christ, there is no point pursuing anything else in life. The kingdom itself cannot be a healthy pursuit apart from first understanding the revelation of our current righteousness in Christ.

I will share one testimony of the power of walking with a paradigm of righteousness. Early this year, my wife and I had the opportunity of meeting regularly with the "Aboriginal Prince of East Arnhem Land" in the Northern Territory—a divine meeting. Bunumbirr and his wife, Vanessa, are royalty in those parts, according to their culture. They are a humble, godly couple with a great love for our nation. They invited us into their lives and family to teach them their identity in Christ. Week after week we sat with this family on their porch, in the heart of their community, teaching them of their righteousness in Christ.

Within two weeks, Bunumbirr had responded so well to the empowerment and intimacy of this message that he had already made leaps and bounds in His relationship with the Father. He had also made a disciple of his own and taught him the same message in his language. That was in March. It is now November. In just a few months, in this isolated region of our nation, Bunumbirr has walked so powerfully in the truth of his identity that he has seen well over eighty people in his community born again and baptized! The message has since reached over one hundred and twenty people, invading surrounding communities too. These growing numbers meet daily—gathering around the truth, worshiping, and dancing into the night—enjoying a real growing relationship with the Father and learning to steward their new lives in Him. Righteousness is being preached and people are rushing into the kingdom to be set free and to walk with God. Because of the reality of the truth, people are being liberated from addiction to gambling, drinking, drugs, fighting, suicide, abuse, and so much more because of satisfaction in their relationship with the Father.

Bunumbirr, being the prince, has a very strong responsibility in the land among the Yolngu people to lead the ceremonies pertaining to various cultural rituals. Some are rooted in the demonic and the worship of creation totems. He has made a powerful stand for one-way living (Jesus plus nothing), rather than a common two-way philosophy where Jesus is acknowledged, but only alongside the various worshiped totems and dreamtime myths (Syncretism).

He has been heavily persecuted for his stand, had spears thrown at him, and had his family threatened with violence. He refuses to lead or even partake in these rituals. If he continues to renounce the demonic aspects of ceremonies in this land, then when he becomes king, the law of the land in his culture will be in his hands to steward. Because of this, he is under immense pressure to partake of the ceremonies of his people. Carloads of men have shown up at his house attempting to pressure and threaten him into ceremonial activities. He has stood his ground with courage and with a deep peace, having learned his authority and power as a son of God, deeply loved by the Father.

The powerful change Bunumbirr's region is experiencing is just one example of the mass global awakening taking place as the church rediscovers this core message of the gospel: righteousness. It is a one-way wave, sweeping across the land and liberating the masses. It's led by people like Bunumbirr and Vanessa—with laid-down lives, established in righteousness, and abounding in love. We can actually walk without offense, in sincerity, and without fear, self-promotion, pride, lust, and so much more. We do this by identifying with Jesus Christ alone as those who have passed from death to life, having been made compatible with God in righteousness. This is not for the occasional Christian; it is for every Christian!

There are over six hundred references to righteousness in Scripture. It is like buying a new car you thought was rare. Suddenly you see the same car everywhere you go! You may like to do a study on righteousness. You will find it most exciting to see how scripturally incorruptible it is.

Righteous is what you have become in Christ so that righteousness can become your natural way of life!

(ENDNOTES)

1. Watchman Nee, The Life That Wins (North Chesterfield, VA: Christian Fellowship Publishers, 1986), 26.
2. Some verses that reference our new nature and the significance of the doctrine of righteousness as the heart of the gospel: Galatians 2:16; 2:20; Colossians 1: 13-14; 2:9-10; 3:3; Romans 1:16-17; 6:6; 3:24; 5:1; 8:30; 5:17,21; 3:21; 10:4; 10:10; 14:17; 4:25; 6:18; 1 Corinthians 1:30; 15:34; 6:11; 2 Corinthians 5:21; 5:17; 3:9; 6:7; 1 John 1:4; Ephesians 4:24; 5:8; Matthew 6:33; Hebrews 5:13; 2 Timothy 3:16; Titus 3:7; Philippians 3:9; Psalms 17:15; Hebrews 10:14; John 16:10; Acts 24:25; 1 Peter 2:24; 2 Peter 1:3-4, 9-10.
3. Hebrew words: H6662. צַדִּיק ṣaḏiyq (206 times), H6663. צָדַק ṣâḏaq (41), H6664. צֶדֶק ṣedeq (116), H6665. צִדְקָה ṣidqâ (1), H6666. צְדָקָה ṣeḏâqâ (157)
4. Greek words: Strong's G1342. δίκαιος dikaios (81 times), G1343. δικαιοσύνη dikaiosynē (92), G1344. δικαιόω dikaioō (40), G1345. δικαίωμα dikaiōma (10), G1347. δικαίωσις dikaiōsis (2), G1346. δικαίως dikaiōs (5)
5. Strong's H6666
6. Strong's G1342
7. Strong's G1343
8. Romans 1:17; 3:22; 10:3-4; 10; 1 Corinthians 1:30; 2 Corinthians 3:9, 5:21; Ephesians 4:24; Philippians 1:11, 3:9; 1 Peter 2:24
9. Strong's G1344

CHAPTER 6
A DIVINE INVENTORY

As we discover we share God's righteousness in Christ, we can explore our new existence in Him. Astounding things have happened in us through our co-crucifixion and co-resurrection with Jesus. We did not just get an entrance to heaven, but a new life with a new nature. Here are seventeen of the many statements in Scripture which prove we have undergone a total change. I often recite these truths out loud to Father God as I pray from a place of thankfulness. You might like to try this too.

- *I have partaken of the divine nature.* | 2 Peter 1:3

- *I am a new creation in Christ.* | 2 Corinthians 5:17

- *I once was darkness but am now light in Him.* | Ephesians 5:8

- *I have become the righteousness of God in Christ.* | 2 Corinthians 5:21

- *I was translated from the domain of darkness into the kingdom of His love.* | Colossians 1:14

- *I am filled with the fullness of God.* | Colossians 2:9

- *I am dead to sin.* | Romans 6:2,7 & 11

- *I am free from sin.* | Romans 6:7,18 & 22

- *I am born of God.* | John 1:12–13

- *I am reconciled to God.* | 2 Corinthians 5:18; Romans 5:10

- *I am regenerated.* | Titus. 3:5

- *I am redeemed.* | Colossians 1:14

- *I am holy, blameless, and above reproach before Him.* | Colossians 1:22

- *I am forgiven.* | Colossians 3:13; Ephesians 4:32

- *I am perfected.* | Hebrews 10:14

- *I am purified.* | Titus 2:14

- *I am currently seated in the heavenly places in Christ Jesus.* | Ephesians 2:6

Pretty amazing, right? All these breathtaking statements clearly reinforce we are not what we used to be.

The Greek word used for "new creation" (2 Corinthians 5:17) is the word *kainos*. You are a *kainos* creation. This does not mean a second chance at your old life in Adam. The word means "of a new kind, unprecedented, uncommon, unheard of."[1] You are a creation that has never existed before. You were made of an entirely different substance when you were filled with God and recreated!

> *"For the death he died he died to sin, once for all, but the life*
> *he lives he lives to God. So you also must consider yourselves*
> *dead to sin and alive to God in Christ Jesus."*
> **ROMANS 6:10-11**

One definition of the Greek word used above for "consider" means "to take inventory."[2] Paul told us we must take inventory of ourselves as dead to sin and alive to God in Christ. How do you take an inventory? It is an assessment of your new nature as a *kainos* creation, checking your stock.

How is your mind? Is it still corrupt from the fall of Adam and full of evil? If not, then why can you still have impure thoughts passing through your head? What about your conscience? Is it still defiled and helpless, unable to accurately tell right from wrong? How about your heart? Is your heart still deceitful above all things (Jeremiah 17:9)? Should you still sing psalms like "Create in me a clean heart, oh God, and renew a right spirit within me" (Psalms 51:10)?

The simplest starting point for this divine inventory is to recognize that as Jesus is, so are you in this world (1 John 4:17), since you are conformed to His image (Romans 8:29). Jesus is not just our Lord, Savior, and the eternal Son of God. He is also our reference for the new life we have been given as we share the divine nature. This is very significant.

The heart is a critical aspect to have clarity on regarding how to have intimacy with God and pursue freedom from sin; as is the conscience— ours to steward in purity, in the same way Jesus modeled, in a relationship with the Father.

THE PURE IN HEART SHALL SEE GOD

The heart is a beautiful theme of Scripture. It means far more than just an organ that pumps blood. The Greek word for heart is *kardia*.[3] The word is used metaphorically in most of the New Testament, just as it is in the Old Testament in the Hebrew language. *Mounce's Expository Dictionary* says: "Kardia covers a whole range of activities that go on within one's inner self, including thinking (Mark 2:6, 8), grieving (John 16:6), rejoicing (John 16:22), desiring (Romans 1:24), understanding (Ephesians 1:18), and decision-making."[4] It is essentially the "seat of moral nature and spiritual life," also known as the "inner man."[5] It breaks down into many various aspects of our inner life, but also commonly represents our entire spiritual life and health. What a great element of our new nature to take an inventory of. If it is still deceitful and corrupt, then perhaps we cannot trust any of its functions.

"Blessed are the pure in heart, for they shall see God."
MATTHEW 5:8

If having a pure heart means we can "see God," then what better aspect of our new nature is there for the enemy to confuse? If he can get us to think the heart is evil and untrustworthy as Christians, then we will live in shame and condemnation, shying away from knowing the Father. Many mention how David cried out that God would create in him a clean heart and a right spirit (Psalms 51:10–14) and wrongly apply this request to themselves. We even sing it in some churches. We must learn to rightly divide the word of truth (2 Timothy 2:15) so we can live in the fullness of our new life in Christ, not in the shame produced by wrongly diagnosing ourselves. David saw his need for a new heart, a great insight under the old covenant and something we all need, but this changes in the new covenant.

"The heart is deceitful above all things, and desperately sick;
who can understand it?"
JEREMIAH 17:9

This verse is also often wrongly quoted. Remember, the new covenant brought a new existence with it. We must understand the context and covenant of the prophets so we can see what they were pointing to. I have too often heard this verse used to challenge people to be careful of the heart. Too many sons and daughters are tormented with introspection and uncertainty because of this confusion. We are supposed to interact with God from the heart and even be moved by the desires of the heart (Psalms 37:4). How can we do this if it is still evil beyond all things?

When studying the heart, both Ezekiel (36:26; 11:19) and Jeremiah (24:7) mention that we will be given a new heart.

"And I will give you a new heart, and a new spirit I will put within you. And I will remove the heart of stone from your flesh and give you a heart of flesh."
EZEKIEL 36:26

"And I will give them one heart, and a new spirit I will put within them. I will remove the heart of stone from their flesh and give them a heart of flesh."
EZEKIEL 11:19

"I will give them a heart to know that I am the Lord, and they shall be my people and I will be their God, for they shall return to me with their whole heart."
JEREMIAH 24:7

In these three verses, God promises to give us a new heart—a heart to know Him. That is the point of the new covenant: to remove the sin issue, restore us to God's righteousness, and give us the relationship with Him every human heart desires. We love to quote the Old Testament prophecies, and rightly so, but we need to quote the right ones—the ones consistent with the new covenant! Also, if the heart broadly represents the entire inner man, then surely we must associate our co-crucifixion and co-resurrection in Christ with our heart too, right? If our old inner man of sin was completely crucified with Christ and we became renewed (Romans 6:6; Colossians 3:3; Galatians 2:20; Colossians 2:11–13), then God gave us a heart transplant in Christ.

Let's look at some statements about the new covenant condition of our hearts.

"The good person out of the good treasure of his heart produces good, and the evil person out of his evil treasure produces evil, for out of the abundance of the heart his mouth speaks."
LUKE 6:45

"Whoever believes in me, as the Scripture has said, 'Out of his heart will flow rivers of living water.'"
JOHN 7:38

Here, Jesus was referencing the indwelling of Holy Spirit we receive. Holy Spirit does not dwell in an impure temple. This includes the heart here. The following two verses also affirm this:

"And who has also put his seal on us and given us his Spirit in our hearts as a guarantee."
2 CORINTHIANS 1:22

"And because you are sons, God has sent the Spirit of his Son into our hearts, crying, "Abba! Father!"
GALATIANS 4:6

"You stiff-necked people, uncircumcised in heart and ears, you always resist the Holy Spirit. As your fathers did, so do you."
ACTS 7:51

Here Stephen rebuked the Jews for being "uncircumcised in heart." He knew circumcision happened to the heart at conversion. God removes the sinful nature/old man and makes us new creations.

"But a Jew is one inwardly, and circumcision is a matter of the heart, by the Spirit, not by the letter. His praise is not from man but from God."
ROMANS 2:29

Here Paul also showed that the circumcision of the old man in Christ included the entire inner man or heart. We are not left with dark corners of the inner man, distinguishable only by God but undiscoverable by us. Jesus gave us a new life and Holy Spirit is longing to draw us into all truth regarding this (John 16:13).

"And he made no distinction between us and them, having cleansed their hearts by faith."
ACTS 15:9

When we put our faith in Jesus Christ at salvation, He *cleanses* our hearts. The Greek word here for cleansed is *katharizo̅* and literally means to "purify, or purge," also "to free from defilement of sin and from faults, to purify from wickedness, to free from guilt of sin, to purify."[6] Peter used this language to explain the conversion experience.

"The aim of our charge is love that issues from a pure heart and a good conscience and a sincere faith."
1 TIMOTHY 1:5

"Having purified your souls by your obedience to the truth for a sincere brotherly love, love one another earnestly from a pure heart."
1 PETER 1:22

Godly love comes from a heart that has been made pure. If we believe we start out with a perverted heart once we are born again, what chance do we have of living pure lives of love? If we believe this, then when the enemy comes with false thoughts and desires to tempt us, we will blame it on an impure heart instead of overcoming the deceptive fiery darts with a revelation of our purity.

"Let us draw near with a true heart in full assurance of faith, with our hearts sprinkled clean from an evil conscience and our bodies washed with pure water."
HEBREWS 10:22

*"So flee youthful passions and pursue righteousness, faith, love, and
peace, along with those who call on the Lord from a pure heart."*
2 TIMOTHY 2:22

You can see here that a part of our salvation package is a new heart,
a heart to know the Lord. Our inner man has been cleansed. This is
another powerful angle of the reality of our 100 percent share of God's
righteousness. It affects our inner man totally. We have a heart we can
authentically love one another from—a heart in position for a holy,
glorious life of love. As we have seen, we must still independently choose
to walk in this purity faithfully. We have a pure predisposition toward
holiness, love, and life now, one that issues from our innermost being.
The enemy can still deceive us though, causing us to partner with impure
or deceptive motives and thoughts as a response to fear or lies we believe.
We do not automatically manifest a pure experience just because He has
purified our inner man. We must live in the fullest expression of our
purity, which is possible through intimacy with God and faith. We must
challenge lies and motives of self-driven expressions the enemy would
love us to adopt.

It is also important to note we are called to steward our hearts in purity.
James mentioned an ability we have to be deceived in our hearts (James
1:28), meaning we can still believe lies that influence the thoughts and
ways of our inner man. To get a little more clarity on stewarding the
inner man, let's look at the conscience.

THE CONSCIENCE

The Greek word translated conscience is *suneidēsis*. It means "moral
awareness." The conscience is a part of the human soul that produces
feelings of grief when we violate it or feelings of pleasure and security
when our lives are in step with our values system. This values system
can be a secular one, an emotional one, or based on any set of perceived

ethics, but the conscience is only in true health when tied to scriptural truth alone and washed clean by the blood of Jesus. It can then keep us in step according to God's truth as we walk with Holy Spirit.

I picture the conscience like a power board. There is a "trip" system on a power board so that if a surge of electricity comes toward the board, the board will "trip," cutting off the current before it can go past the power board and damage the appliance being powered. The conscience is like a trip switch for the inner man. Before a temptation, lie, or action can violate your values and govern your behavior, your conscience will signal that if you enable these temptations to identify you, you are crossing a line into something that will bring death instead of life. You are responsible for deciding whether you let the surge through with your will.

As Christians, we must learn to walk with a clear conscience, which grows in strength and sharpness by growing in scriptural truth. It then functions in bringing this truth to remembrance in our practical life and our thought life. This is why we must become mighty in our knowledge of the Scriptures. Martin Luther used his conscience as an incredible defense when refusing to recant his teachings against the heretical practices of the Roman Catholic Church:

> *"My conscience is captive to the word of God ... to act against conscience is neither right nor safe."*
> **MARTIN LUTHER**[7]

How blessed the bride is that Martin Luther honored his conscience, paving the way for doctrinal health in the modern church. When we grow in the revelation of truth and our conscience becomes our safeguard, we can address issues before they cause us to dishonor every part of ourselves—offering them to sin instead of righteousness and functioning as less than we are (Romans 6:13).

A hindrance to a holy, intimate lifestyle can be what the Bible calls a seared conscience. The blood of Jesus sprinkles us clean from an evil conscience when we are converted (Hebrews 10:22; 9:14), making us naturally inclined toward holiness as we grow in understanding. However, we can sear the conscience by not stewarding it in purity (1 Timothy 4:2). This is when our ability to discern moral evil from good in our relationship with God is compromised by persistence in sin, at the cost of the outcries of our conscience. It is like when Play-Doh becomes hard and stubborn on its exterior when it has not been used for some time, and needs to be massaged back to softness. This can happen to our conscience if we do not use it properly.

Have you ever had a strong sense of wrongdoing when you first gave in to a temptation to sin? Like: you knew you were giving parts of yourself over to something they were not designed for, thereby submitting your value to something unfitting? Like: you lose your temper or give yourself to lustful desires. If it is ongoing and unaddressed, you can harden the senses and the clarity of your conscience. The degree of wrongdoing does not change, but the conscience is no longer as sharp in detecting this and preserving a practice of holiness. It does not trigger your conscience as much over time if you sear it. If you do not keep this in check, you can subtly excuse sinful patterns. Be careful. God calls us to walk with a clear and soft conscience, motivated by the desire for pure intimacy with Him (Acts 23:1; 24:16; Romans 13:5; 1 Timothy 1:5; 1:19; 3:9; 1 Peter 3:16; 3:21).

> *Even though you have been given an entirely new nature,*
> *it is yours to honor.*

It is especially devastating when people associate with a message like righteousness and then live consistently sinful lives, without remorse or conviction, because of a seared conscience and a resulting lack of desire to know and walk with the Father. This requires a revelation of the devastation of sin and God's hatred toward it, a deeper understanding of our created value, and honest repentance.

Claiming righteousness as an excuse to ignore sin, rather than to walk away from it, is a sin.

When you understand the lengths Jesus went to in setting you free, you will develop such a value for your freedom that you'll actually learn to hate sin. If you feel you may have seared your conscience, are you willing to see this for what it is and walk back into purity? If so, then right now, Jesus will reorientate your conscience in a moment—if you invite Him to—softening it immediately by His grace and walking you into practical holiness, in line with your new holy nature again. Humble yourself and lean on His love and truth. I frequently pray to Holy Spirit, "Help me to steward my conscience in purity and sensitivity, in honor of the blood of Jesus shed for the redemption of my life. I was bought at a price. I choose to live in softness and truth before you."

"For godly grief produces a repentance that leads to salvation without regret, whereas worldly grief produces death."
2 CORINTHIANS 7:10

It is important to make something clear as we learn to steward our consciences. There is a difference between worldly grief and godly grief. Worldly grief is rooted in condemnation and a misunderstanding of God's heart toward us. It is limited in bearing real fruit and damages our relationship with God. Godly grief, however, comes from the realization we are living in less than our true inheritance of holiness and union with Christ. Our conscience triggers this in our heart. Godly grief leads to repentance and freedom, with no regret or condemnation. Many Christians have not experienced a life without regret or condemnation because they are only familiar with worldly grief. It is godly grief which keeps our relationship with the Father intact, while still confronting sin we may deal with and walking us into freedom from it. It becomes a joy when we discover an area we have failed to steward in our new lives, because we know the result of addressing this is a deeper connection to the Father and a clearer conscience. It will leave us with no condemnation or regret. Godly grief can be a discomfort, but it is a liberating thing when our desire is to live transformed lives. It happens relationally, by the love of the Father, while Holy Spirit orientates our conscience toward a more attentive holiness by the blood of Jesus wherever needed. It feels good to crave for His holiness to manifest in our lives!

I pray that my message is clear. In no way am I promoting a life of sin or denial, but an actual freedom from sin because of the reality of righteousness. If you are living in habitual sin and you feel sorrow for it, desiring to be free from it, then you are well positioned for freedom. The fact you wish you never did it, and still feel grieved when you sin, proves you are a new creation, no longer compatible with that way of life. You are repentant and desperate to manifest your freedom and honor God because you love Him! It shows your conscience is crying out according to your growing understanding of your new life. If you lean into intimacy, transparency, and the truth, the Father will rapidly love you out of sin and into holiness. Let Him nurture you in the reality of your right standing with Him, removing condemnation so you can remain in a place of closeness to Him—a place where sin becomes distasteful as your conscience is softened and aligned to truth. Agree with God that He has delivered you from every ounce of authority sin once had in your life. You are a powerful person, responsible and able to walk in liberty in Christ.

The function of our new nature is subject to our desire to walk it out.

Here are a few of many examples of how the apostles lived and taught in the way of a good conscience:

> *"And looking intently at the council, Paul said, "Brothers, I have lived my life before God in all good conscience up to this day."*
> **ACTS 23:1**

> *"So I always take pains to have a clear conscience toward both God and man."*
> **ACTS 24:16**

You can see in the two above verses that Paul attempted to conduct his life toward God and man with a clear conscience, knowing how it pleased God and facilitated intimacy and love.

> *"I am speaking the truth in Christ—I am not lying; my conscience bears me witness in the Holy Spirit."*
> **ROMANS 9:1**

This indicates that intimacy with Holy Spirit is a way to be confident you are living with a clear conscience.

> *"For our boast is this, the testimony of our conscience, that we behaved in the world with simplicity and godly sincerity, not by earthly wisdom but by the grace of God, and supremely so toward you."*
> **2 CORINTHIANS 1:12**

When we steward our conscience well in the truth, we behave as godly people, because that is what our cleaned conscience trains us to do. As you can also see in this verse, this godliness works by the grace of God, not religious striving.

> *"The aim of our charge is love that issues from a pure heart and a good conscience and a sincere faith."*
> **1 TIMOTHY 1:5**

"They must hold the mystery of the faith with a clear conscience."
1 TIMOTHY 3:9

"Having a good conscience, so that, when you are slandered, those who revile your good behavior in Christ may be put to shame."
1 PETER 3:16

A good conscience produces good behavior.

"Pray for us, for we are sure that we have a clear conscience, desiring to act honourably in all things."
HEBREWS 13:18

When we live with a clear conscience, we will act honorably in all things.

"How much more will the blood of Christ, who through the eternal Spirit offered himself without blemish to God, purify our conscience from dead works to serve the living God."
HEBREWS 9:14

When we walk with a clear conscience, we do not act with the motive of appeasing a violated conscience or earning a right position with God (dead works), but rather of honoring God and bringing Him glory, as one who is already made like Him and responding in love.

I originally sought to write about sharing the mind of Christ or the soul realm here, but I cannot risk being mistaken for sharing a message that does not get real. I pray I am not associated with a message that does not produce real holiness and a pure conscience, motivated by intimacy with the Father rather than fear or religious striving. There is no condemnation in my words if you have been in the place of a seared conscience or complacency toward sin, but rather (in these words) I hope you read an invitation to recognize the truth about you, to let your conscience be sharpened, and to walk into something far greater.

Imagine a company of people who live without violating their consciences, knowing they have been given an incredible redeemed compass for moral and spiritual life. As new creations, we can learn to be governed in practical life by a pure conscience, steered by healthy new covenant convictions as we grow in relationship with the Father. These convictions result from the scriptural revelation we feed our souls, found within intimacy with God.

In the new covenant, we are called to function in relationship with God, pursuing a way of living in the royal law of love that Christ brought to light and keeping a clear conscience, according to the purposes we discover in Him for our new life.

If knowing the truth sets you free (John 8:32), freedom must be a barometer for what you perceive to be biblical truth.

(ENDNOTES)

1. *Strong's* G2537
2. *Strong's* G3049
3. *Strong's* G2588
4. Precept Austin. "Heart - Kardia (Greek Word Study)." www.preceptaustin.org/heart_kardia.
5. Blue Letter Bible. "Heart/Heartily." www.blueletterbible.org/search/dictionary/viewTopic.cfm?topic=VT0001335.
6. *Strong's* G2511
7. R.C. Sproul, *The R.C. Sproul Collection Volume 2: Essential Truths of the Christian Faith / Now, That's a Good Question!* (Carol Stream, IL: Tyndale House Publishers, Inc., 2017).

CHAPTER 7

THE DECEITFULNESS OF SIN

"If I am not a sinner anymore, why can I still sin?"

This is a question we must consider. If we have undergone such a drastic internal change, why can sin still be so prevalent in our lives? As new creations, we still have an ability to sin, to the same degree that we had an ability to sin before we were born again. But by understanding the "deceitfulness of sin" (Hebrews 3:13) and what sin is, we are further empowered to recognize and walk away from it. Knowing the truth about sin helps us to understand what is happening if we are tempted or give in to sin's deception, and know how to avoid it. Here is a good statement to remember:

Jesus became an entire human being to redeem the entire human being.

As we have seen, we are righteous now. We have no sin in our nature. God has worked an incredible work in our entire being. This must inform the way we view sin and the way we view God's whereabouts about us. Many of us have made a devastating mistake of considering sin to be an *indwelling* reality, while God remains distant. *It is the opposite!* God lives inside us now, intimately and actually, while sin is on the outside. This simple change of view can bring immense freedom. Sin can still very much be an issue in our lives though. While we know sin is no longer ruling us from the core of our nature, how does sin find influence, how we can preempt it, and how we can live free from it?

For those who would say, "We must have part sin in our nature or we would not sin," I ask, did Adam and Eve have a sinful nature when they sinned and ate from the Tree of Knowledge of Good and Evil? No. They were made in the image and likeness of God, with no sin in them. They were completely pure but could *choose* sin when tempted by an *external* enticement. Just because we are free from a sinful nature now, it in no way removes our ability to choose sin. That is why Paul says to "not let sin reign in your mortal body" (Romans 6:12). Sin is no longer in our mortal bodies, but we can still let it reign there and obey its desires, producing sin in our lives. It is time to expose the greatest crime syndicate of all time—the *entity of sin*.

You were born with a nature that you could not choose (sinner), then born again with one you could not earn (saint).

THE NOUN THAT FOOLED US

Vine's Expository Bible Dictionary gives insight into numerous verses that present sin as a "personality," an independent power, as not just *actions* we do, but an *entity* we engage with. See this definition:

A governing principle or power, e.g. Romans 6:6, "(the body) of sin." Here "sin" is spoken of as an organised power, acting through the members of the body, though the seat of "sin" is in the will (the body is the organic instrument); in the next clause, and in other passages, as follows, this governing principle is personified.[1]

Wow! Sin is a personified force. A *noun*.

The two most prevalent Greek words used for sin are *hamartanō* (verb)[2] and *hamartia* (noun).[3] In the book of Romans, for example, the verb is used only twice; the noun, however, is used forty-six times!

If this entity is no longer an indwelling one, what happens when we let it reign in our mortal bodies (Romans 6:12)? Imagine there was a young lady named Stacy who, for many years, had an abusive, manipulative husband. She lived trying to please him, but he was never happy with her. He did not let her leave the house much, and he made her feel as if she had no value. He was controlling, manipulative, and very negative. Her behavior was dictated by his broken conclusions of who she was. After living this way for such a long time, Stacy could hardly remember what normal relationships were supposed to be like. She felt stifled, like she was no longer herself, yet was afraid to leave because of what her husband might do.

One day, Stacy's husband wrote her a horrible, accusatory, suicide note: his final attempt to rule her life. He then took his life. A sad illustration, but a similar thing happened to a friend of a friend. Now, you would think Stacy would have come out of this season and moved on in freedom, no longer at the mercy of this terribly deceived man. However, she still rarely went out of the house. She still behaved as though she was carefully trying to please her husband. She was no longer married to him but continued behaving as if she were. She lived as though she were walking on eggshells, compulsively keeping the house immaculate, cooking his favorite meals, and still behaving as if she had no value. Her husband was "reigning in her mortal body," determining the actions of her day-to-day life, even though he no longer had authority or power in her life.

This is what it is like to let sin reign in your mortal body. When sinful desires, accusations, or thoughts dictate your actions and thought life, they are reigning in your body. This does not mean you take on a sinful nature again. It means you have let the thing Jesus delivered you from have a say in your life again and produce sin. The Message Bible illustrates this well:

> *"So what do we do? Keep on sinning so God can keep on forgiving? I should hope not! If we've left the country where sin is sovereign, how can we still live in our old house there? Or didn't you realize we packed up and left there for good? That is what happened in baptism. When we went under the water, we left the old country of sin behind; when we came up out of the water, we entered into the new country of grace—a new life in a new land!"*
>
> **ROMANS 6:1–3 MSG**

Also:

> *"When Jesus died, he took sin down with him, but alive he brings God down to us. From now on, think of it this way: Sin speaks a dead language that means nothing to you; God speaks your mother tongue, and you hang on every word. You are dead to sin and alive to God. That's what Jesus did.*
> *That means you must not give sin a vote in the way you conduct your lives. Don't give it the time of day. Don't even run little errands*

*that are connected with that old way of life. Throw yourselves
wholeheartedly and full-time—remember, you've been raised from the
dead!—into God's way of doing things. Sin can't tell you how to live.
After all, you're not living under that old tyranny any longer. You're
living in the freedom of God."*

ROMANS 6:10–14 MSG

We are new creations now, free from a sinful nature; however, the entity
of sin is still in the world. It comes from outside and challenges us with
thoughts and desires for sin that are not ours. When we believe they are
our thoughts and desires, we often give in to them and produce sin.

Before we sin as an action (verb), we let sin (noun) reign in our mortal
bodies from the outside first, "obeying *its* passions and desires" (Romans
6:12). To make it even clearer how sin is personified in Scripture, let's
read a few verses from Romans 7, replacing the noun *hamartia* (sin) with
the human name Larry:

> *"But Larry, seizing an opportunity through the commandment,
> produced in me all kinds of covetousness. For apart from the
> law, Larry lies dead. I was once alive apart from the law,
> but when the commandment came, Larry came alive and I
> died. The very commandment that promised life proved to be
> death to me. For Larry, seizing an opportunity through the
> commandment, deceived me and through it killed me."*
> **ROMANS 7:8-11**

You can see here sin is defined as far more than "missing the mark," or an
action we perform. It is also an external personified force. We were previously
united to this entity in our nature as sinners, but we are separated from it
when we believe the gospel. Sin still exists outside us, however, trying to
influence us and keep us in bondage. Sin's aim is to use our mortal bodies
as instruments to express itself (Romans 6:13, 19), tempting us to choose

sin, robbing Jesus of the glory we are called to display for Him in purity. Picture sin like an active radio transmission the enemy puts out, emitting background noise in our world's atmosphere—a type of broadcast, sustaining brokenness by keeping people in darkness and deception. As Christians, we no longer naturally speak sin's language, and we must learn not to associate ourselves with the broadcast—the subtle thoughts and temptations. The less we identify ourselves by sin's sound, and the more we identify ourselves by our new life in Christ and set our minds on things above (where the broadcast is not even present), the less we will submit to its sound.

Many of us have mistaken the desires and thoughts from the entity of sin for our heart's desires and thoughts, wrongly concluding we remain impure after conversion. We have associated the desires or thoughts we experience toward sin as part of the old man, even though the Bible states inarguably the old man is dead. We call it a "remnant" or "echo" of the sinful nature, the "flesh," or other perceived unregenerated aspects of the soul realm. In reality, its source is a separate, personified force called sin.

Look at the first time in the Bible where sin is mentioned. God had just refused Cain's offering but accepted Abel's. When God observed Cain's anger, God said:

> *"If you do well, will you not be accepted? And if you do not do well, sin (chatta'ath)⁴ is crouching at the door. Its desire is for you, but you must rule over it."*
>
> **GENESIS 4:7**

Sin is crouching at the door? *Its desire* is for you? Again, sin is presented as a whole lot more than merely an action we do. Now look at the same verse again, but in the King James Version:

> *"If thou doest well, shalt thou not be accepted? And if thou doest not well, sin (chatta'ath) lieth at the door. And unto thee shall be his desire, and thou shalt rule over him."*
>
> **GENESIS 4:7 KJV**

The King James Version takes an even more accurate approach to the Hebrew wording in this verse by saying "*his* desire," naming sin as a personified force with desires and temptations. The Hebrew word for "desire" here means "desire, longing, craving ... of a beast to devour."[5] What a sinister thing sin is, with such evil desires to rule over that which belongs to God.

HOW DOES SIN WORK?

As it relates to Christians, sin is an external, personified force that has no power over us anymore, except by two ways:

1. The Power of Sin Is the Law (1 Corinthians 15:56)

Sin tries to deceive us into believing we do not measure up to God's standard of righteousness. This forms a "house divided against itself" identity (Mark 3:25) because we perceive some darkness *and* light in ourselves. We then strive to fix the darkness on our own, because we identify ourselves by sin's deception. When we do this, we are far more likely to give in to the temptation.

> *Sin aims to get you striving for what God already fulfilled in you by grace.*

Sin wants us to perceive ourselves as less than sharers of God's righteousness and then to divide ourselves in our mindset as both light and darkness. If we believe the lie we have not been made entirely righteous in Christ, we will try to earn it on our own, the thing *the law* compelled us to do. It is in this pursuit that sin will come and we will naturally believe its passions and desires are ours. As you see in the next verse, sin gains power through the law.

"The sting of death is sin, and the power of sin is the law."
1 CORINTHIANS 15:56

The truth that will disarm this strategy of sin is:

"For sin will have no dominion over you, since you are not under law but under grace."
ROMANS 6:14

This does not mean you should live in sin because you are under grace. It means you should live *free from sin* because you are under grace! We are already fully redeemed and righteous by grace and are not bound to the old covenant law. Here are more verses on this:

"For Christ is the end of the law for righteousness to everyone who believes."
ROMANS 10:4

"Do we then overthrow the law by this faith? By no means! On the contrary, we uphold the law."
ROMANS 3:31

"Now we know that the law is good, if one uses it lawfully, understanding this, that the law is not laid down for the just but for the lawless and disobedient, for the ungodly and sinners, for the unholy and profane, for those who strike their fathers and mothers, for murderers, the sexually immoral, men who practice homosexuality, enslavers, liars, perjurers, and whatever else is contrary to sound doctrine."
1 TIMOTHY 1:8–10

"Do not think that I have come to abolish the Law or the Prophets; I have not come to abolish them but to fulfill them."
MATTHEW 5:17

Jesus fulfilled the requirements of the law for us. He then made us wholly like Him under the new covenant. When we become steadfast in this truth, sin loses its ability to grip us with its temptations, and our actions are transformed. Sin can no longer hold us to the standards of the law, condemning us for not reaching them, spiraling us into sinful behavior.

2. Deceitful Desires

Another way that sin tries to gain access to us is by tempting us with sinful desires (or emotions) that are not ours, hoping we will believe the desires are ours, especially because in the past we produced these innately. We now have reorientated desires through our purified heart and have received the mind of Christ (1 Corinthians 2:16), inclining us intuitively toward holiness in our thoughts and desires. Sin tries to cause us to second guess this reality and take on flawed ways of thinking and feeling, leading to flawed and sinful actions.

As Christians, we can often distinguish thoughts that go through our minds and acknowledge not every thought we have is ours, but many of us still identify with every single *feeling* we *feel*.

The truth about this is:

Desires for sin are deceitful, not defining.[6]

Sin's desires do not *define* you; they are trying to *deceive* you. They are an external enticement, challenging your identity and fighting for you to conceive with them and produce sin. Knowing not every desire you feel is yours makes dealing with deceitful desires a lot simpler. Without this realization, we can quickly become introspective and confused when we encounter feelings contrary to our new nature, believing they are always ours. We then question the simple truth that we are light with no darkness, or the effectiveness of the finished work of Christ in our lives, rather than engaging faith and truth against an external, deceitful desire.

Here is a question I heard Holy Spirit ask me one day as I was grappling with my identity and finding my way toward this truth: *How fast must you run to outrun yourself?*

If you think feelings and thoughts toward sin are originating from your fundamental desire to sin, you will fight against yourself to become pure. You're not finally pure once you stop *feeling* or *thinking* about sin; you're pure because of the Bible's declaration you have been purified in Christ (Titus 2:14). Outrunning yourself is impossible; that is why God crucified your old self with Christ. You must stand on the truth that you *already are pure,* and the truth will reign in your expression because the lie has been exposed.

If you believe you are light and have no darkness in you, like the Bible says, then deceitful desires are easily exposed. They will lose their volume and impact in your life as you build yourself in your relationship with the Father and in truth, guarding you against any sin trying to deceive you. Temptations can become more obviously distant than you may ever have thought possible. Have you ever heard the saying "You cannot stop the birds flying overhead, but you can stop them from nesting in your hair?" Temptation is like a bird flying overhead, showing up on your radar in the air. Do not let them land. You do not have to. In fact, as you continue to walk in this single-minded view of your new life in Christ, even the overhead temptations come to feel further and further away from you, increasingly distinguishable as foreign entities.

WHAT ABOUT JAMES 1:14?

> *"But every man is tempted, when he is drawn away of his own lust, and enticed. Then when lust hath conceived, it bringeth forth sin: and sin, when it is finished, bringeth forth death."*
> **JAMES 1:14–15 KJV**

What is James saying here? Does he suggest we have natural evil desires for sin still, originating from within, even without the help of sin or the devil? The above is quoted from the King James Version. The word "lust" instead of the word "desire" was chosen for the translation. At a glance, it can appear we have a fundamental lust for sin. However, the Greek word used for lust here, *epithymia*, is a *neutral* word for "desire."[7] It is a word that can mean basic human desire, healthy desire, or evil desire, depending on the context it is used in and how it is interpreted. This is important to distinguish.

Because of an unfortunate translation of the word in the KJV, many have concluded this usage is one of inherent *evil* desires, making a case for a remaining sinful nature in Christians, or at least an impure heart. However, many modern translations use the neutral word "desire," a more accurate choice (NKJV, NLT, and ESV, for example). Let's look at it in the NKJV:

> *"But each one is tempted when he is drawn away by his own desires (epithymia) and enticed. Then, when desire has conceived, it gives birth to sin; and sin, when it is full-grown, brings forth death."*
> **JAMES 1:14–15 NKJV**

To conclude the word for "desires" represents evil ones here, thereby translating the word as "lusts," can only be added into the verse through our interpretation of the neutral Greek word. Look at this verse in Luke, where Jesus had the same desire:

> *"And he said to them, "I have earnestly desired (epithymia) to eat this Passover with you before I suffer. For I tell you I will not eat it until it is fulfilled in the kingdom of God."*
> **LUKE 22:15-16**

Did Jesus have *"evil* desires" to eat Passover with His followers? Of course not. He *"earnestly desired."* As we can see, this Greek word for desire can be used for good and evil desire.

So what was James describing here? As Christians, we were regenerated with desires inclined toward holiness. Through the purifying work of Christ, we are empowered to direct and exercise these with self-control. This is why, when we are not living with a seared conscience, we feel bad if we sin. We are not designed for it anymore. James explains here how our basic human desires can be "enticed" by the enemy and they can conceive evil, producing sin. Satan attempts to "draw away" our desires, enticing them into sin, through deceitful temptations.

Where can we get insight elsewhere in Scripture, showing James is describing the dynamics of temptation for new creations? Whose life can be an example of how external enticement toward sin works for someone who does not have a sinful nature? There are two scriptural examples that apply perfectly to James's description: Adam and Eve (Genesis 3:1–7) and Jesus (Luke 4:1–12). Neither had sinful natures, but both experienced a direct temptation and enticement to sin exactly as James described. In both cases, the enticement for sin was 100 percent external.

As we know, in Adam and Eve's case, Eve's desire eventually "conceived" with the external enticement of the devil (Genesis 3:6). What happened then? *"When desire has conceived, it gives birth to sin; and sin, when it is full-grown, brings forth death"* (James 1:15). James nailed it. This is exactly what happened to Adam and Eve. This was almost identical to Paul's explanation of Adam and Eve's fall in the garden, "Sin came into the world through one man, and death through sin" (Romans 5:12). This is a description of pure people, enticed by an external temptation, giving in and producing sin. For Christians, likewise, temptation is an external enticement. Notice here God held Adam and Eve personally responsible for their sin, not the devil. The devil was responsible for the deception and the temptation, but Adam and Eve were to blame for their sin. Once we conceive with sin, it is our responsibility, as He recreated us in Christ with the ability and authority to withstand temptation and live free from sin. This is important to recognize. We cannot blame the devil for our sin if we stumble.

In Jesus's case (Luke 4:1–12), His desires were also enticed by an external temptation in the desert, but He did not give in and therefore remained pure. This account teaches us it is not a sin to *experience* temptation, nor does temptation define us. Jesus "in every respect has been tempted as we are, yet without sin" (Hebrews 4:15). It is *obeying* temptation that is a sin. Also, have you ever considered the devil was possibly not appearing to Jesus in physical form here? There is no evidence it was physical. Perhaps it was in the same way he approaches us, invisibly, with thoughts, desires, accusations, and lies.

We are just the same as Jesus is in this world (1 John 4:17), conformed to His image (Romans 8:29) and partakers of His nature (2 Peter 1:4). Therefore, the account in Luke 4 where Jesus, having all the same basic desires we do, was enticed by external temptations from the devil, is the same dynamic we experience when sin tempts us. James, knowing this well, explained what happens when someone with a pure nature is enticed, not someone with a sinful nature. James did not write his epistle apart from the foundational understanding that Jesus Christ lived as an example for our Christian lives; therefore, we must understand James 1:14 through this same simple truth. James commented here on how sin tries to operate in our lives with the knowledge that we are like Christ.

Where Adam and Eve failed in the garden, giving in to the external temptation of sin and conceiving sin, Jesus was victorious. Because He stood firm in the truth, these enticements from the enemy could not conceive with His desires for Him to produce sin. This was not an inner battle Jesus had to fight, but one He won by standing in the truth of the Scriptures in the face of external temptations.

"*When desire has **conceived**, it gives birth to sin*" (James 1:15). How many parties are required to conceive? At least two! This was James's point. Your desires are being enticed by *external and deceitful* temptations from the power of sin and the devil. If you give in, sin conceives with your desire, causing you to produce sin instead of holiness.

James was not making the grim and contradictory conclusion of a lifelong inner battle between purity and impurity here. This would deny the explicit message of the gospel. He was rather empowering us to live free by recognizing the enemy's craftiness. He was warning us about how our desires and thoughts can be led astray and enticed by the external temptations of the devil. "Know your enemy," he essentially told us. Protect your desires and stand in the truth, following Christ's example. Be self-controlled against the temptations of the devil by knowing the truth and walking in your identity. Satan longs to conceive and give birth to sin in our lives, dishonoring and waging war against the holiness of God.

DON'T EAT THE GARBAGE!

I was preparing for a day of prayer and fasting once. I did what I always do: I cleared my schedule, turned my phone off, and planned my hours of reading the Word, journaling, praying, and enjoying intimacy with God. This is the joy of my life! I feel deep satisfaction in being intentional to know the Father. Nothing will ever prove more valuable in our lives than this. Christine was set to go off to work for the day, so I could have the whole day to be alone with my King.

However, during the night before my intentional day, I had a vivid, perverted, sexual dream. I had not yet realized my inner man was not the issuing source of these dreams, feelings, and perversions. I awoke to a whole bevy of feelings—guilt, lust, temptation, distraction, and evil desire. I knew enough of my identity to believe God had set me free from sin, at least theoretically. However, I still associated the dream and the feelings with some hidden corner of my nature that was still dark, still generating and craving such things. Rather than taking authority over my dream life and putting my mind on the truth about me, I identified by the dream and tried to fight against what I perceived were my desires.

I subtly believed these were still somehow my desires, but having what felt like an equal desire to spend the day with the Lord, to know Him, and honor Him, I fought the feelings of lust, tried to shake the dream off, and set out to pray and study the Scriptures. Around midday, I realized I had spent most of my morning trying not to give in to sin by struggling to ignore the strong feelings of lust. I was reading the Bible extra hard, more as a defense mechanism against sin than a launchpad for intimacy with my Father!

In my frustration, I had a real moment with God. "God, I put this day aside to intentionally be with you. Half the day is gone now, and I feel all I am really doing is *trying not to sin*." My eyes had been scanning Scripture for hours, but my mind was primarily occupied with trying not to give myself to this lustful temptation I thought was mine.

Many who read this will relate. You want to be with Him, to honor Him, to live pure, but those feelings are strong. It's difficult to perceive these temptations as an external enticement, especially if you have struggled with something like pornography for years previously as a sinner with an inherent sinful disposition. Holy Spirit spoke to me in that frustrated moment, clear as anything, "What if it is not you?"

As He spoke, a sudden realization dropped into my heart. A divine clarity exposed the temptations as being completely separate to me, like fiery darts being thrown at me rather than my desires from within me. Just like Jesus's temptation recorded in Luke 4 and Adam and Eve's in the garden, the enemy was trying to entice me into sin with these feelings and thoughts. I had believed a lie that deep down, in an undiscovered or unconverted facet of my nature, beyond the reach of Holy Spirit's regeneration, there was a perverted, lustful desire I had not dealt with—a lie that I still wanted to look at pornography almost as much as I wanted to know God. This thought alone was filling me with guilt, even before I had given in to the temptation. In the past, this guilt then usually drove me to eventually give in, which would cause more guilt and a cycle of sin.

I struggled to be honest and intimate with the Father because I still defined myself by the dream and the desires. The moment He spoke, though, Scriptures rushed through my head about freedom from sin, verses that describe sin as an *outside* enticement before they become a personal, conceived action; Scriptures about not letting sin reign in my mortal body (Romans 6:12), and about the deceitful desires of sin and the devil (Genesis 3:1–7; Luke 4:1–13; Ephesians 4:22; 1 Peter 1:14; Romans 6:12; Hebrews 3:13).

It clicked. I stopped trying to fight the feelings as though they were mine. Instead, I acknowledged out loud to the Father that my new nature did not want sin or lust anymore, I was a man of holiness and purity, clean in my mind and my heart, and there was only light with no darkness in me. Immediately the lie was exposed, the truth manifested, and the deceitful desire disappeared! Sin was aiming to rule me, but I ruled over it in the truth, setting my mind on things above, where my true life is hidden with Christ in God (Colossians 3:1–3).

Let this sink in. The sin you may have been battling for years that you can't seem to overcome was overcome by Jesus on the cross. There is a familiar feeling, a deceitful desire, or a wrong thought pattern trying to rule you. When you move from a place of expectation that you will always struggle with these desires to a place of determination to change your mind to accept the truth, you can change your behavior and expose these temptations. When you recognize the ways of the enemy and do not define yourself by the desires anymore, they lose their ability to reign in your mortal body.

Picture this. Striving not to sin as a new creation is like trying really hard not to chew garbage from the trash can. It becomes a lot easier when you realize and believe you no longer naturally like garbage! Then you can ignore it and walk free from it without fighting a perceived inner battle against something you don't want. Too many Christians are striving not to eat "garbage" because they think and feel like they want to eat it! Who wants to eat garbage? You are a new creation with new fundamental desires in your innermost being. Any striving that we Christians do against sin should only be against the external deceptions of sin (Hebrews 12:1–4), girding up the loins of our minds (1 Peter 1:13) and leaning into the Father's faithfulness. He can keep us from giving in or losing clarity (1 Corinthians 10:13).

Your fundamental desire is for Him, not sin.

Here are a few of many verses that present sin as an external and separate entity to us as new creations:

> *"Therefore, since we are surrounded by so great a cloud of witnesses, let us also lay aside every weight, and sin which clings so closely, and let us run with endurance the race that is set before us."*
> **HEBREWS 12:1**

Sin here is referred to as "clinging closely," not occupying our nature or indwelling us.

> *"Beloved, I urge you as sojourners and exiles to abstain from the passions of the flesh, which wage war against your soul."*
> **1 PETER 2:11**

Here, sinful desire is referred to as the passions of the flesh, which are waging war *against* our souls (mind, will, and emotions), not from within our souls (also Hebrews 12:4).

"Let not sin therefore reign in your mortal body,
to make you obey its passions."
ROMANS 6:12

Here, we see sin desires to reign in our bodies, but it is not in our mortal bodies. As we saw, we have the power to not let sin control our actions and thought lives by causing us to think it still has a say, like Stacy did with her deceased husband. We also see here sin has its *passions*, these are the passions we previously believed were ours when we felt them, but now we can discern them as deceitful desires and not give ourselves to them.

"By which he has granted to us his precious and very great
promises, so that through them you may become partakers of the
divine nature, having escaped from the corruption that is in the
world because of sinful desire."
2 PETER 1:4

The corruption in the world is from sinful desire. We are free from that corruption now, and the sinful desire that causes it. Remember, sin did not just enter Adam, it entered *the world* through Adam (Romans 5:12). It is no longer in us as we are in Christ, but it remains in the world. We must recognize the difference.

"What shall we say then? Are we to continue in sin that grace
may abound? By no means! How can we who died to sin still
live in it?"
ROMANS 6:1-2

We died to sin (also Romans 6:7, 11). We are also *free* from sin (Romans 6:7, 18, 22). That includes freedom from its passions and desires.

"And those who belong to Christ Jesus have crucified the flesh
with its passions and desires."
GALATIANS 5:24

Here we are told we have crucified the flesh (flesh being synonymous with the sinful nature in this verse) with its *passions and desires*. The evil passions and desires of our old, sinful nature do not hang around once we are new creations. The passions and desires of the entity of sin, however, are still in the world. Now we only walk in and desire sin because we adopt wrong ways of thinking or feeling.

You are not the sum of the thoughts and feelings you encounter. You are the sum of what Christ achieved on the cross and what Scripture declares about you. When you fight for the definition of Scripture alone, you can walk in the freedom you have always desired.

Temptations for sin originate from the enemy's fiery darts and the entity of sin, not from indwelling impurities. This is why in Ephesians 6, Paul strongly invited us to put on the armor of God against these fiery darts of the enemy. Why wear armor to protect ourselves from these darts if the battle starts on the inside? It is the external battle against sin we are engaged in.

Please note, I am not denying or ignoring the reality of the demonic in this chapter. I am focusing on the dynamics of sin, a commonly overlooked aspect of the invisible realm. The demonic plays a part in reinforcing sinful habits, and they can try to oppress Christians in a variety of ways. We overcome demons by the same faith we overcome anything in the Christian life: by the truth and power of God, we have power and authority over the demonic realm in Christ, the same way we have authority over sin.

A HEBREWS 3:13 CULTURE

> *"But exhort one another every day, as long as it is called 'today,'*
> *that none of you may be hardened by the deceitfulness of sin."*
> **HEBREWS 3:13**

As some good friends and I have learned the truth about what sin is, the reality of living free from it has become a far more consistent experience in our lives. It requires intentionality, intimacy, and humility, but is nonetheless available. We do not always get it right, but we pursue the fullest expression of this from intimacy with God. This is not motivated by legalism either. Grace and Holy Spirit empower freedom.

We are cultivating what we call a "Hebrews 3:13 culture." This helps us pursue the enjoyment and multiplication of powerful freedom from sin. This has not only been pivotal to our freedom. As we reproduce this culture in our ministries and communities, many are also experiencing a new quality of transparent relationship and freedom from sin.

We "exhort one another" constantly, reminding and inviting each other into the fullness of who we are in Christ, speaking the truth over each other. We will not let the deceitfulness of sin harden us and cause us to shy away from intimacy with God or openness with each other. If we feel sinful temptations, or anything we do not see in the life of Jesus, we recognize this as a deceitful desire originating from the entity of sin. Often it goes away when we internally process it with Holy Spirit, holding it up to the truth. If not, we expose the lie out loud with a friend and remind each other of the truth about us. Exposing the lie and elevating the truth then extinguishes the deceitful desire and our susceptibility to it.

We do not believe the lies we encounter in our thoughts or feelings originate from ourselves as new creations. We take the declaration of our purity in Scripture seriously. Because of this, we can freely and humbly expose lies without identifying with them. This thwarts the enemy's attempt to guilt and condemn us into remaining confused or in secret sin.

It is very important to remember the standard of our relationships and communities is not perfection, but it is humility. This helps eliminate secrecy and hypocrisy because of an unhealthy, corporate expectation of perfection. We do not expect people to be perfect, even though we believe practical freedom from sin is possible. Instead, we expect people to be humble and transparent. We encourage people that by a proper understanding and the empowerment of grace, we can live holy and humble lives. By "setting our minds on things above" (Colossians 3:2) and refusing to let the desires of sin define us, we can overcome sin in our lives!

As we awake to our new holy life in Christ all across the planet, we will witness an unprecedented purity.

Cultivate a Hebrews 3:13 culture among your friends and family. It will change the way you perceive sin, keep you sharp against deceitful desires, and breed a deeper quality of relationship with those you love.

A final thought: Sin is nothing to be nonchalant about. It is the oldest form of "spiritual warfare," yet rarely perceived as such. It is the enemy's greatest weapon. Sin provokes you to shame, guilt, and condemnation, all deliberate obstacles to prevent you from engaging with God in intimacy. It ruins relationships, hardens hearts, and destroys lives. Sin is not okay. We live in a culture that consistently broadcasts a complacency or lack of value toward living in holiness. We must remain vigilant in our perspective of sin and seriously pursue purity in the church.

God hates sin as much today as He always has. Sin ridicules His holiness and His design for humanity. It challenges His dominion and His goodness on the earth. The church of our generation must fight for a high standard of holiness. We must show the world the pure and holy nature of God in a more powerful way than ever.

He set you free from sin for a reason. You can live a holy life. He is worth it.

Do not mistake the age of mercy we currently live in for an age of leniency toward sin on God's part. You can, and you must, pursue freedom from sin.

(ENDNOTES)

1. e.g., Romans 5:21; 6:12, 14, 17; 7:11, 14, 17, 20, 23, 25; 8:2; 1 Corinthians 15:56; Hebrews 3:13; 11:25; 12:4; James 1:15
2. *Strong's* G264
3. *Strong's* G266
4. *Strong's* H2403
5. *Strong's* H8669
6. Genesis 3:1-7; 4:7; Luke 4:1-13; Ephesians 4:22; 1 Peter 1:14; Romans 6:12; Hebrews 3:13
7. *Strong's* G1939

CHAPTER 8

THE MISSING LINK

A righteous nature. A pure heart. One spirit with the Lord. Holy and free. Empowered to walk free from the deceitfulness of sin. What an inventory. The new you is so beautiful that you can be intimate with God in union with Christ. But how can all these beautiful truths about you be real if your experience falls short of them? Many reasons why we do not live in the fullness of the gospel have been decided among Christians.

Here are a few:

> *"I am not holy enough."*
>
> *"I need more grace."*
>
> *"I need to be more anointed."*
>
> *"I am only positionally righteous."*
>
> *"My 'flesh' is too strong."*

"I just resurrect the old man too often."

"The devil is just too good at limiting me."

"God's will is still a mystery, so I cannot know for sure who I am or how to live."

The Bible gives none of these reasons. It does not try to limit your salvation to a positional tease or a future inheritance. It does not leave you just a couple of "tools" short of living the Christian life. The reality of God's nature is living inside you. You have all things for *life and godliness* right now (2 Peter 1:3). You come short in *no* gift (1 Corinthians 1:7). You have *every* spiritual blessing (Ephesians 1:3).

There is a missing link though. We can't deny it. The experience of our new life is not instant. The Bible speaks about the missing link constantly, but we rarely view it as the thing we need. What can help us pursue this missing link; what can help us make the truth about us become our experience?

> *"My people are destroyed for lack of knowledge; because you have rejected knowledge."*
> **HOSEA 4:6**

Lack of knowledge? Is it that simple? This verse does not say God's people are destroyed because the devil is too powerful, or because God has hidden His will from them, or because they are sinners. Lack of knowledge or rejection of knowledge destroys us.

> *"And you will know the truth, and the truth will set you free."*
> **JOHN 8:32**

Looking closely at this oft-quoted verse, you will see that the truth does not set you free—*knowing the truth* sets you free!

> *"And so, from the day we heard, we have not ceased to pray for you, asking that you may be filled with the knowledge of his will*

in all spiritual wisdom and understanding, so as to walk in a manner worthy of the Lord, fully pleasing to him, bearing fruit in every good work and increasing in the knowledge of God."
COLOSSIANS 1:9-10

Paul never stopped praying that people would have the knowledge of God's will, and that they'd receive it with wisdom and understanding. He did not pray they would become more sanctified, more anointed, get more impartation, or get more grace. It is spiritual *understanding* that causes you to "walk in a manner worthy of the Lord ... bearing fruit in every good work." Understanding who you are in Jesus and choosing to believe it causes you to live what you are.

"I do not cease to give thanks for you, remembering you in my prayers, that the God of our Lord Jesus Christ, the Father of glory, may give you the Spirit of wisdom and of revelation in the knowledge of him, having the eyes of your hearts enlightened, that you may know what is the hope to which he has called you, what are the riches of his glorious inheritance in the saints."
EPHESIANS 1:16-18

Paul prayed the same thing for the church in a different region: that the saints would have wisdom and revelation in the knowledge of God, and that they would know the inheritance living inside them! He did not pray they would *receive* their inheritance, but that they would *know* the one they already had.

"The beginning of wisdom is this: Get wisdom, and whatever you get, get insight."
PROVERBS 4:7

"My son, if you receive my words and treasure up my commandments with you, making your ear attentive to wisdom and inclining your heart to understanding; yes, if you call out

for insight and raise your voice for understanding, if you seek it like silver and search for it as for hidden treasures, then you will understand the fear of the Lord and find the knowledge of God."

PROVERBS 2:1-5

Understanding is more precious than gold and silver, more cherished than treasures of wealth and riches. Wisdom itself is that we would pursue wisdom and insight. The Lord knows that what we believe determines not just how we think, but how we live too. This is why we must cry out for understanding.

"And it is my prayer that your love may abound more and more, with knowledge and all discernment."

PHILIPPIANS 1:9

How do you abound in love more and more? Is it by receiving something from God you do not already have? No. Grow in accurate knowledge of God and you will grow in love as a response to His beauty.

"And I pray that the sharing of your faith may become effective for the full knowledge of every good thing that is in us for the sake of Christ."

PHILEMON 1:6

When you have the full knowledge of every good thing in you, then sharing your faith becomes effective. Having had an ecstatic heavenly encounter can't do that, despite their being exciting, available, and helpful. An encounter will help you to know God's glory and nearness, but you are no less empowered to live like Jesus if you do not have one.

"This is good, and it is pleasing in the sight of God our Saviour, who desires all people to be saved and to come to the knowledge of the truth."

1 TIMOTHY 2:3-4

Guess what? God does not just want you to be saved. He wants you to be saved *and come to a knowledge of the truth*. A knowledge of the truth is how you can see evidence and enjoy the fruit of your salvation.

I could go on here, but you get the picture. A common missing link is *understanding*. We need to *know* the truth so it can set us free. That is why I am taking the time to write this book. It is why I pursue putting the truth of our new life in Christ into simple words. I need not stroke my ego, or be known for having great revelation. I desire to see masses of people liberated by proper understanding. When we get understanding and live vigilant and self-controlled lives, we can finally walk in the fullness of the truth.

Sometimes we can be so hung up on our sinful behaviors that we struggle to put our attention on the truth long enough for it to make a real difference in our lives. Imagine you and I were at a café together, and I held up a big green flower of broccoli in front of you. Imagine I then stated, "Don't think about broccoli for the next ten seconds." What would you be thinking about for that ten seconds? Even if you managed not to think directly about broccoli, you would still think about not thinking about it! Too many of us are trying to not focus on sin rather than putting our attention fully on the truth that makes us free. I am not telling you to ignore sin. I am telling you the way to real freedom is in putting your attention on the truth, which makes you free.

> *We best address sin by becoming diligent in understanding the truth.*

You do not need more grace; He has lavished you richly with it (John 1:16; Ephesians 1:7–8). You do not need something extra for life and godliness (2 Peter 1:3). You must get understanding. The flawed things we believe about ourselves as Christians are not cute discrepancies. Our lack of knowledge destroys us (Hosea 4:6). It robs us of the life we are called to manifest. We must change our minds about ourselves and pursue a proper understanding of who we are. Through intimacy with God, we must pursue the manifest reality of the truth.

If you don't see freedom in your life, the purity of your perspective should be questioned, not the purity of your nature.

INTIMACY-BASED UNDERSTANDING

Let me clarify some things. When the Bible speaks of knowledge or understanding, it is not limited to academic or intellectual knowledge. To pursue knowledge, it is not necessary to trot off to seminary for seven years. The source of pure knowledge, the knowledge of God, comes from intimacy (Proverbs 2:6–7), intimacy not one human being is shut off from. It has an intellectual aspect, but its true source is intimacy, not academia.

This is an important distinction to make, especially in the West. We have developed an idol of intellect in much of our secular society. As Christians, we must not fall into the trap of pursuing an intellectual understanding of theology to find a sense of identity rather than knowing the person of God and rooting our identity in Him. We should pursue understanding from a place of intimacy and acceptance in the Father. This way our lives will be transformed, not just our vocabulary.

True understanding transforms your life, not just your vocabulary.

There are multiple Greek words used to describe understanding. Many of these words do not stop at the intellect, although the intellect is certainly involved. The Greek words such as *ginōskō,* imply an *"experiential understanding."*[1] *Strong's* explains this word was even used as a "Jewish idiom for sexual intercourse between a man and a woman." This is the same type of word as the Hebrew word for "know" (*yâḏa*), which was used for such expressions as "Adam *knew* Eve, his wife, and she conceived and bore Cain" (Genesis 4:1). This shows true biblical knowledge has a tangible and real impact. It is a thing of intimacy, not just intellect.[2]

Another reason intimacy is the root of understanding for Christians is that "all the treasures of wisdom and knowledge" are hidden in Jesus Christ Himself (Colossians 2:3).

Christian knowledge should be inseparable from the person in whom it is found.

Paul's strongest pursuit in life was to know Christ Jesus. Everything else was trash to him. Paul wasn't interested in pursuing academic knowledge, but a rich, experiential knowledge of God, the only kind which can transform lives and lead to an increasing quality of intimacy with God.

> *"Indeed, I count everything as loss because of the surpassing worth of knowing Christ Jesus my Lord. For his sake I have suffered the loss of all things and count them as rubbish, in order that I may gain Christ."*
> **PHILIPPIANS 3:8**

Was Paul against being intellectual or against understanding society, theology, and culture? Of course not. He used his intellect on many occasions to explain the gospel (Acts 24:25; 26:1–32; 28:23). He rarely did this, though, apart from a demonstration of God's tangible power too. If we do not let our understanding produce the reality of God in our lives, we may wind up defending the gospel intellectually with no experiential evidence that convinces people of His reality.

> *The gospel should be powerfully displayed and intellectually explained. It was never meant to be intellectually defended void of a tangible expression.*

Theology is an incredible gift. We must pursue understanding about who God is and who we are. But if we ever remove this gift of theology from its intended environment of intimacy, we will become puffed up and wrongly find our identity in it. True knowledge and wisdom are *in Christ*, and it is Holy Spirit who desires to lead us into all truth (John 16:13). We must think of understanding as an intimate thing *and* a cognitive thing. If we can talk people into the gospel with our incredible intellects, they are at equal risk of easily being talked out of it again. It is an intimacy-based understanding— tangible intimacy *and* intellectual understanding—that, when displayed, compels other people to know God. Ultimately, it is the blood of Jesus that reveals our acceptance, approval, and value—not our ability to retain or regurgitate information.

AN INHERITANCE FULLY ATTAINED BUT LARGELY UNSPENT

Imagine you meet up with a good friend for coffee. This friend goes way back with you. He loves you deeply and has incredible trust in you and your destiny. You trust and love this special friend. You have not been doing so well financially, finding yourself in a tight spot. Your generous friend knows this. While you are enjoying your coffee and spending quality time together, your friend slips $10,000 into your jacket pocket while you are not looking. A crisp bundle of cash. He desires to bless you abundantly and see you succeed at life; he knows this will help you do that. Your friend was unaware you did not see him slip this money in your jacket, so you go on enjoying your time together.

Now imagine you finish meeting with him, pay for your coffees, and then go your separate ways. Now, because you do not *know* your friend has done this, does that mean the $10,000 is not real? Of course not. It is sitting in your jacket pocket right now.

Your knowledge of something does not determine its reality.

The same goes with your inheritance in Christ. Just because you have not known or experienced that it is fully given right now, does that make it any less real? That is a silly conclusion, but Christians conclude this about their inheritance every day.

Now imagine you go home, take your jacket off, and hang it up in your closet. A week or two goes by before you pull it out again, put it on, and go out again to meet other friends. You still have not seen the money! Let me ask you this: Have you been $10,000 richer for that whole two weeks? And at what point did that $10,000 become yours fully? In reality, it is no longer your friend's from the moment he gave it to you. It has been your $10,000 since the moment it landed in your pocket! You are $10,000 richer than you were two weeks ago.

Because you did not *know* it was sitting in your pocket the whole time, you lived *exactly* like you did before you received the $10,000. You may have even argued over a twenty-dollar meal bill with some friends during that time. Believing you were broke, you lived like a broke person. This is the experience of many Christians. They believe one day they will receive an inheritance as saints and sons, not knowing it has already been given! Our inheritance is too often lying dormant, fully available but undiscovered.

Now imagine a whole month has gone by. You are wearing your jacket yet again. You reach into the pocket to look for your phone and what do you find? $10,000! You finally discover your friend's gift. Now you have *knowledge* and *understanding* of your $10,000. This means you can finally enjoy your gift! You could not spend it until you knew it was there. The same goes for your inheritance in Christ. You have immeasurable power, authority, freedom, liberty, blessing, faith, grace, and access to the Father right now! It is time you enjoyed your inheritance.

Imagine one more helpful scenario: You are yet to discover the $10,000 sitting in your jacket pocket. You believe your generous friend wants to give you $10,000, but you feel you must earn it from him. Surely you cannot just expect him to give it to you for nothing? You go to his house once a fortnight and mow his lawns. You babysit his kids while he takes his wife out on a date. You even wash his cars for him. Now, remember, you had the $10,000 the whole time, but you did not know it. You work for it for years, wondering when your friend will finally give it to you.

As time goes on, you even doubt his generous spirit and intentions as a friend. Meanwhile, he sits in his living room watching you mow his lawns, wondering why you never spent the immense gift he gave you or even thanked him for it. This is another position many Christians find themselves in—working for the things already fully given, all because of a huge misunderstanding. The Father really is a generous friend.

FAITH MEETS EXPECTATION

> *"Now faith is the assurance of things hoped (expected) for, the conviction of things not seen."*
> **HEBREWS 11:1**

One Greek word for hope can also mean confidence or expectation.[3] One aspect of faith is that it meets your expectation, *but* your expectation is determined by your understanding. Let me explain.

If I read the Scriptures and *understand* I can heal the sick, I rightly *expect* (hope) I can lay my hands on the injured cashier at the store and see her healed. My *faith* will meet my expectation. Faith, which is the *evidence* of things unseen, will manifest as I pray for her and she will be healed. If I do not understand my authority, I am not likely to pray for her at all. If I pray but do not expect healing to manifest, it probably won't. Simple and challenging, right? Your faith meets your expectation.

As we grow in understanding, we can trust the word of God and act accordingly with what we discover about ourselves. Faith can then manifest according to the truth. We expect the things of our inheritance because we've learned it has already been given to us.

As I learned I was free from sin (Romans 6:7, 18, 22), I expected freedom from long-term struggles with lust, selfishness, and insecurity. Guess what manifested? The truth. I got free from things I never imagined I could be free from. Then I came to understand (intimate knowledge, remember, not just cognitive) I was accepted in the beloved, loved by the Father, and made like Him—all for the sake of intimacy with God. I expected I would have an intimate and dynamic relationship with the Father after years of condemnation and confusion. Guess what manifested? The truth. I have a manifest peace before God, I have experiential access to Him, and I know He loves to be with me. Because I understand this, I am learning to constantly apply it, and I do not believe lies that would try to tell me otherwise. My faith meets my expectation. I am enjoying my inheritance.

Do not let your experience determine what you believe is true. Let the Scriptures determine the truth. Take the truth you read about to prayer and let your experience become transformed by it. In all your getting, get understanding (Proverbs 4:7). Do not perish for lack of knowledge; the mystery has been revealed. It is Christ *in* you, the hope (confident expectation) of glory (Colossians 1:27).

A key attribute of this awakening to righteousness is that limiting paradigms in our understanding are being removed. We have realized there is nothing stopping us from enjoying our inheritance in Christ right now. We are not *growing* in purity, holiness, or Christlikeness, we *already* are alive in these things in Him. We are growing in understanding and intimacy. We are no longer easily deceived, tossed to and fro by every wind of doctrine (Ephesians 4:14); we finally see the manifest *evidence* of our new life in Christ. But what can our daily lives really look like in Jesus?

(ENDNOTES)

1. *Strong's* G1097
2. *Strong's* H3045
3. *Strong's* G1680

CHAPTER 9
LIVE LIKE HIM

What can our lives look like as righteous saints, sons, and daughters? Where can we look for an accurate example?

Jesus is the one who makes us what we now are. But we did not share in His death and resurrection and then go our separate ways. We have been united with Him in a profound way. It is *in* Him that we exist. We are united to Him now and for all eternity. Our new nature is in total dependence of our union with Him. Jesus made us one spirit with Himself through His death and resurrection (1 Corinthians 6:17).

When you discover you have become like Jesus, conformed to His image (Romans 8:29), as He is (1 John 4:17), and made one spirit with Him (1 Corinthians 6:17), it is necessary to rethink what Jesus represents for you now. Does He represent an unattainable standard you will always fail to meet? Is He the substitute for your punishment of sin and the fulfillment of the law alone? Or is He also the *example* of your new life in Him?

Previously in my Christian walk, I only shared my flimsy faith in half-drunk arguments with unbelievers as I lived in complacency and behaved like an orphan. Since grasping righteousness, though, and being inspired by many normal Christians walking in their inheritance, it has been a pleasure to grow into a deep and real relationship with the Father that affects the world around me.

A few close friends and I cultivated an expectation that the reality of God would manifest as we came to understand our identity in Christ. We put the truth in practice and sought to take God at His word. We have since seen thousands of miracles, *following us* as we pursue to *know Him*. We also have the privilege of equipping other people to walk in the same identity and power, simply by changing their minds about who God is and who they are. There was the time where countless hundreds were healed in the secular marketplaces of West Timor in Indonesia. Multitudes were responding to give their lives to Jesus. Tumors vanished and blind eyes, deaf ears, and crippled bodies were instantly restored. There was the time when we traveled to gang-heavy areas of New Zealand after having a vision in prayer, and we saw countless healings, encounters, and lives surrendered to the living God as we went on an international "treasure hunt," looking for the Father's treasure—the people He longs to redeem.

There are times when the restaurant staff come out from the back kitchen of the place we are eating, one by one, to receive healing. Entire hotel lobbies become sickness-free areas. There are healings that happen over the phone across the world, or people request prayer from overseas, leading to lives being committed to Jesus. There are the New-Agers and Muslims on the streets meeting the God who created them through power encounters, healings, and love. Legs grow out and broken bones are healed. People have divine encounters where "a voice" speaks clearly to them, and then they come to where we are because they were specifically directed there by this voice. There are the *schoolies*, school leavers who are out to party and celebrate finishing high school—on the Gold Coast and other cities—encountering God and rushing into the kingdom by the hundreds. Visions, deliverance, miracles, and the glory of God manifesting everywhere!

There is "The Jesus School," a discipleship ministry we started with Youth for Christ Australia. One school had thirty-five students in a community environment for ten days. During the school, over fifty people encountered God and were born again! There were public baptisms and radical miracles. This was mostly at the hands of the newly-empowered students, not the leaders.

As we emphasize identity and relationship with God, evangelism becomes a spontaneous success. As we continue to run these schools, more and more are coming into their identity and walking in righteousness. Another recent Jesus School in Darwin, Northern Territory, was capped at sixty students, who spent two weeks of their time learning their identity and putting it immediately into practice, with huge fruitfulness all over the Territory. We just ran our most recent school in South Australia, again capping numbers in order to strategically pursue intimate and total transformation for people in a discipleship environment. This school saw such momentum around this message of righteousness that we rented the local town hall to accommodate the hundreds of people gathering to worship Jesus and enjoy His presence. Miracles and salvations broke out and a potent culture of liberty was embraced. Multitudes hit the streets to share their faith and heal the sick. An article was written in the local secular paper about this wave of disciples who descended upon the area, with photos of miracles printed for all to read. Jesus was glorified. We are learning the simple and powerful reality that:

The gospel works!

The kingdom is manifesting in increasingly diverse places too, as we learn to expect more and to be ourselves in our different spheres. My wife, a doctor, sees patients and coworkers healed as she walks in simple love and faith in her medical profession. Miners working in rough environments are seeing many encounter Jesus. We must see His love invade every aspect of society, not just limit ourselves to traveling evangelism. When you know the King, the kingdom continually manifests.

Once you discover His profound reality in the place of intimate relationship, you will develop an insatiable hunger to see His reality displayed to the world around you. I am learning to cultivate and savor this drive for His reality.

These testimonies are just from a handful of friends and me. I hear constant stories from other people of tens of thousands coming to know Jesus through this supernatural Christlike life, all over the world. Every day, countless people are encountering God and becoming sons and daughters. Normal Christianity will never look the same again.

Jesus is the example, not the exception.

JOEL SHAW

Jesus modeled God's original design for humanity, to be lived out in right relationship with the Father. He modeled how we, as sons and daughters, can express His very life now, united with Him in a world which needs to discover His love.

We live in Him so we can live like Him!

JESUS – THE ORIGINAL CHRISTIAN

Have you previously compared yourself to the twelve disciples when you read the gospels? Have you defined yourself by their actions, or made excuses for brokenness in your life by pointing out the brokenness in their lives? Then let me point out that in the four gospels, none of the disciples were born again yet. There is only one person who was comparable to a Christian in the Gospels: Jesus Christ. Let me explain.

For His first thirty years, Jesus's ministry was to fulfill the old covenant law perfectly, which He did. His remaining three years, however, were a completely different second ministry. For example, have you ever thought about why Jesus was baptized by John the Baptist? Did he need forgiveness of sins? Of course not. Even John the Baptist protested Jesus's request for baptism, wrongly thinking Jesus was coming to baptize him. Jesus responded to John:

> *"Let it be so now, for thus it is fitting for us*
> *to fulfill all righteousness."*
> **MATTHEW 3:15**

Jesus's baptism represented His death and resurrection. It represented the death of a person who had fulfilled all the righteousness of the law, finishing man's end of the old covenant requirement. Now He could begin His new covenant ministry. This second ministry was to model what a human being, in a right relationship with the Father and free from sin, could look like. Here is the process Jesus went through:

- He fulfilled all the righteousness the law demanded of us (Matthew 3:15).

- He was water baptized, symbolizing His death and resurrection (Matthew 3:13–17).

- He then was filled with the Spirit (Luke 3:22; 4:1, 14).

Jesus became the first born-again, water-baptized, and Spirit-filled new-covenant Christian! Yes, He was fully God and fully man, the eternal Son of God, but He modeled the power and love of the normal Christian life as a man for His final three years. He modeled a life of tangible union with Father God and in understanding of truth, all empowered by grace. From the day He emerged from the desert in the power of Holy Spirit, His entire life ministry changed. He gathered disciples to train in the truth, preached the kingdom of heaven and repentance, and displayed the love of God wherever He went (Matthew 4:17; Luke 3:23). Why did He never have disciples for His first thirty years? Because He had no intention of discipling people to obey the old covenant law. Rather, as soon as He modeled the new covenant, He gathered disciples to equip them in this same way of life!

Jesus is the truth about you, period. Once you are a new creation, looking at Jesus is like looking in a mirror! He is the only person in the entire universe who you should look at to find your true definition and identity.

> *We must not define ourselves by the actions of the disciples in the Gospels. Instead, we must discover ourselves in the person of Jesus.*

RIGHTEOUS FOR A REASON

Let's look at some Scripture that proves Jesus is our example, not the disciples. If you have compared yourselves to the lives of the disciples all this time, this will be a challenging shift, but a necessary and liberating one. It is perfectly scriptural that you are exactly like Jesus now, making Him your obvious example.

> *"Whoever says he abides in him ought to walk in the same way in which he walked."*
>
> **1 JOHN 2:6**

God made us righteous for a reason—not to transform our language and help us set up a "righteousness camp," or so we can talk as Jesus talked. We are righteous so that we can "*walk* as He *walked*." Take notice that this verse does not say to walk as *Peter* walked. Jesus is our ultimate example, not Peter, James, or John.

> *"For to this you have been called, because Christ also suffered*
> *for you, leaving you an example, so that you might follow in*
> *his steps. He committed no sin, neither was deceit found in*
> *his mouth. When he was reviled, he did not revile in return;*
> *when he suffered, he did not threaten, but continued entrusting*
> *himself to him who judges justly."*
>
> **1 PETER 2:21-23**

Jesus was our example. How? By committing *no* sin. Hold on. No sin? Yes. No sin. He was also our example by never having deception in his motives, never reviling when reviled, and by trusting the Father constantly. These are not things we have always seen Christians walk in, but I believe it will become normal Christian practice in our day because of the global paradigm shift that is happening.

We must be empowered to live this way as Christians, or this passage would have called Jesus our substitute, not our example. His first ministry of completing the law on our behalf was His substitutionary work; His second ministry was our example and invitation to live the new covenant life. Gone are the days where a few holy, consistent Christians are the exception in the church. The priesthood is waking up to its identity and walking in understanding. We are empowered in our new nature to follow in His steps. He has not given us an unattainable standard here, but an empowering invitation as those who have been made like Him.

As I said earlier, the standard for Christians is humility, not perfection. Remember, manifest holiness does not save us, the blood of Jesus does. However, the blood of Jesus also *makes* us holy, so I will not lower the standard Scripture sets for the Christian life, no matter the cost. I will uphold and elevate grace as the thing that empowers the Christian life though, by the work of Holy Spirit, so that no one falls into works or legalism. Real holiness is our inheritance.

> *"By this is love perfected with us, so that we may have confidence for the day of judgment, because as he is so also are we in this world."*
>
> **1 JOHN 4:17**

As Jesus is, so are we in this world. We are not like Thomas, the disciple; we are like Jesus. Not in the next world either, in *this* world. This is a great way to check if you believe lies about yourself. Ask yourself if you see your questionable symptom in Jesus's life. Is Jesus depressed right now? No. Then if you are depressed, it is an illegal experience. You are "as He is." Define yourself by the Father's acceptance alone; be released from a spirit of heaviness as you learn to wear the garment of praise in the *truth* (Isaiah 61:3). Is Jesus addicted to pornography right now? No. Then you do not have to look at it *ever* again. Change your mind (repent); you are a powerful person. Draw near to God and walk free. Is Jesus full of fear? No. Then fear is an enemy of your inheritance. Take it on in intimacy with the Father. Perfect love will cast it out (1 John 4:18). The reason you can live as Jesus lived is because you are *as* He is. If you see Jesus walking in power, then you are a powerful person. If you see Him living in freedom, then you can too. Act naturally. Be yourself.

> *"Truly, truly, I say to you, whoever believes in me will also do the works that I do; and greater works than these will he do, because I am going to the Father."*
>
> **JOHN 14:12**

How can we do the same works as Jesus and greater? Because we are made in the same image and nature He is. God predestined us to be conformed to the image of His Son so that Jesus might be the firstborn among many brothers (Romans 8:29). We are brothers with Him, heirs with Him, and sons of God. This means much more than a Sunday song we might sing; it is a huge deal. The whole fullness of God dwelt bodily in Jesus, and we have been filled with that fullness in Him (Colossians 2:9–10).

If you still want to compare yourself to the disciples, that is fine. Just do it once they are born again and filled with the Spirit of God, as you are. Do it from the book of Acts onwards. Peter led three thousand men to Jesus on his first day as a Spirit-filled Christian! Sometimes the disciples prayed for multitudes of sick people, and they were not just from Jerusalem either; people streamed in from the surrounding regions too. Every single one of them was healed (Acts 5:16). This was after Jesus had ascended. This is the church functioning in its inheritance. Once Holy Spirit arrived on the scene and led the disciples into all truth (John 16:13), they finally learned who they were and what they were capable of, making them look a lot more like Jesus. We live in the same season they did. Nothing has changed about the power and love we have access to.

THE KINGDOM OF THE SON

"A new commandment I give to you, that you love one another: just as I have loved you, you also are to love one another. By this all people will know that you are my disciples, if you have love for one another."

JOHN 13:34-35

Even though the miraculous and the power of God is very exciting, let's never forget the main thing: The best example Jesus gave us was not power; it was love and fellowship with the Father. Jesus invites us to deeply acknowledge, receive, and find peace in His perfect love. That way we can truly represent Him well to the world around us as the spontaneous result of our intimacy with Him.

Ultimately the greatest thing Jesus displayed to the world was the love of God. Eagerly desire the gifts, but *pursue love* (1 Corinthians 14:1). As we discover our true righteous identity in Christ, the manifest love of God should become the church's most recognizable trait. Jesus says the world will know His disciples by their love (John 13:34–35). Yes, we will walk in power, purity, and miracles galore, but love should ultimately transcend and overshadow it all. It is love that will win nations. Love never fails.

*Jesus **did** miracles, but He **was** love!*

"Your kingdom come, your will be done, on earth as it is in heaven" (Matthew 6:10). It has become a mantra to the modern church, and rightly so, as establishing the kingdom is our ministry now. But please remember, heaven is not just a kingdom of power and miracles. It is also called the kingdom of the "Son of His love" (Colossians 1:13). We can believe sickness will be healed on earth because there is no sickness in heaven, but let's consider there is also no gossip in heaven. There is no dissension, division, greed, selfishness, arrogance, self-promotion, or pride in heaven. If we really want the earth to look like heaven, let's maintain a well-rounded view of what heaven is *actually* like. Here is a good way to tell if you're seeing heaven manifest on the earth: If you cannot see it in Jesus's life, then it is not in heaven. Take greed, for example. If you cannot see it in Jesus's life, then it need not be in your life. If you can see generosity in Jesus's life, then it can be in your life. That is how we bring heaven to earth. We establish the kingdom in our lives. The kingdom is referred to by Paul as "righteousness and peace and joy in the Holy Spirit" (Romans 14:17). This is far more than miracles, although it also definitely includes the miraculous. It is a life full of the fruit of the Spirit, oozing with intimacy with God through righteousness.

*What is the point of pursuing the kingdom if you
don't actually know the King?*

CALEB BOWLES

The message of righteousness does not just give powerful weapons to spoiled sons and daughters. It forms people of immense character, consistency, intimacy, and love. Do not fail to believe for the fullness of His life in your life. Do not sink into a limited view of how you can truly live. Let's see heaven come to earth in *every* way.

Jesus will always be the example, not your leader, your friends, or your family. We must take our example from Jesus, not the person we know who can best teach righteousness and who functions powerfully in certain areas. Be inspired by people, absolutely, but let them point you to Jesus. Let them remind you that the way Jesus lived defines your inheritance.

*The way to live like Him is to live "in" Him. The
spontaneous result of the value you place on this union
will be a strong resemblance to His life, so focus on
union, not uniformity.*

As a global bride, we are walking into an unprecedented demonstration of power and love on the earth. Our job is to keep our eyes on Him as the true inheritance of the saints in the light. This is how we will see diversity sustained and celebrated in the church. We can all look different from each other, yet all look just like Jesus at the same time.

Public preaching is not the only way to look like Jesus and live a bold life of love. You can embody His love in the workplace: as a doctor, a miner, a farmer, or in any way your redeemed personality in the Lord so inspires. Do not cookie-cut the dynamic ways God wants to bless the world around you through your life. Don't buy a robe, quit your job, and move to Israel to mimic Jesus. Live in the relationship with the Father that He modeled for you. Live in the attitudes and habits of holiness and love He so beautifully demonstrated. Let every area of your life function in freedom, letting your true destiny take shape naturally as you prioritize knowing Him.

We must not let the enemy condemn us. Jesus's life is an exciting invitation, relationally sustained. It is not a standard that condemns us but one that exhorts us in who we truly are. He is a mirror for who we are, not a measure of what we're not!

> *Authentic Christian activity is the spontaneous result of intimacy with God. Become familiar with the Father, or you may make an idol of outreach in our increasing "priesthood" culture to find your identity. Do "not stir up or awaken love until it pleases" (Song 2:7).*

CHAPTER 10
ALL WILL KNOW HIM

I have sinned.

Even since understanding and growing in the truth of righteousness, I have missed the mark. I have given myself to selfishness at times. I have sometimes failed to see people the way God does. I have not revealed His perfect love every day of my life. I have believed lies and lived less than the life of Christ at times. I have occasionally violated my conscience, even if I have quickly repented. If it makes you uncomfortable or irritated that I am so honest and aware of where I have "missed it," you may be wrongly receiving this message.

Let me be clear. My revelation of righteousness does not cause me to live in denial or ignorance of sin if it happens. Instead, it helps me to confront lies with truth, always expecting more holiness and a stronger walk with the Father as I lean back on my identity in Christ. Don't get me wrong.

Compared to my Christian life before understanding righteousness, I now live a life holier than I ever imagined I could. I am more consistent than I ever fathomed was possible, and effortlessly empowered by grace (as we will examine soon). I live free from fear. I *never* experience offense toward anyone in my heart. I am not given to pride. I am a good husband. I am not self-conscious. I am not defined by anything apart from my Father's acceptance—no ministry title, no person's praise, no accusation. My motives for my actions are pure before God. I know Him, and I love those around me well. I do not have hidden agendas with people. I have laid my life down for Jesus. This message changes everything. But I know there is more manifest holiness and love available, and I will never hide from areas I want to see more change or consistency in as I become stronger in the truth and my relationship with God.

I want to talk about the main thing. Please pay careful attention here. This is the point of it all. The times when I miss it are not necessarily the times when I forget my revelation of truth, although this can be a reason. But the times when I sin are more often the times when I neglect the relationship with the Father that my revelation facilitates. Too often, we replace a *relationship* with *revelation*, instead of letting revelation nurture and complement a relationship with the Father.

As we conclude part 2 of the book, I want to exalt the ultimate purpose of the Christian life: The *reason* for revelation is to know God.

Do you know *how* Jesus lived a life completely free from sin? Your answer might initially be that it was because He never had a sinful nature. This used to be my answer too. As we saw earlier, though, Adam never had a sinful nature either before He ate from the tree, but he still sinned. Similarly, Christians all over the world do not have sinful natures but can still live in sin. So how did Jesus do it? It was *possible* for Jesus never to sin because His nature was not conducive to a sinful life. The same goes for us. But what *kept* Jesus from sin was His value for a *relationship* with the Father. The same goes for us.

In His entire thirty years of life before His baptism by John, only one thing Jesus said was recorded in Scripture:

"Why were you looking for me? Did you not know that I must be in my Father's house?"

LUKE 2:49

Jesus was twelve years old. He had been lost by His parents. When they found Him in the temple three days later and asked why He had not left with them previously, this was His response. These are the only words we heard from God incarnate for thirty years of His human life. Imagine that. God walked the earth, and for thirty years we got one sentence! That baffles me. They are profound words because they reveal that Jesus knew God as His Father. They also show He prioritized His relationship with the Father above everything.

Remember, Jesus was fully man and fully God. He was tempted in every way, but was without sin (Hebrews 4:15). He had the same capacity to sin as we do. Was it because He had the perfect revelation that He never sinned? No. The Bible tells us Jesus had to grow in wisdom and stature (Luke 2:52). It was not His wisdom and revelation that kept Him from sin, it was His intimate trust relationship with the Father that He never compromised.

Relationship is built on trust. It was when Adam broke trust with God, trusting the devil instead, that He removed himself from the relationship with God that had kept him free and sustained the clarity of his identity. When you dwell intimately in the Father's love and His thoughts toward you, you are not easily deceived by lies. Never believe the lie that freedom from sin results from revelation alone. Freedom from sin is ultimately sustained by intimate relationship. Revelation can help, but ultimately it exists to facilitate the relationship.

Here is something worth remembering:

> *Your revelation is only as good as the*
> *intimacy with God it produces.*

If you want to live free from sin, use your revelation to know why it exists. *Know God.* He is the one who preserves you; He is the one who is faithful to keep you from sin.

WORTHLESS WIRING AND RUSTING CARS

Your revelation of truth is like the electrical wiring in a wall. It is an internal wiring. You cannot see it is even in the wall. The only way to know the wiring is installed and functioning is if the lightbulb the wiring leads to is shining. The wiring is only as valuable as the light produced from the bulb it is powering! If the light is off, the wiring is worthless. When the light is on, the wiring is effective and useful.

The light in this illustration represents your intimacy with God. Your revelation is only wiring, helping to power intimacy and flood your home with light. You can keep the "switch" to the *on* position by acknowledging the nearness of God, reveling in His tangible love constantly, communing with Him in perfect union, and meditating on the truth. Give yourself to the Father in prayer and worship. Use your revelation for its purpose. Keep the light on.

Another way to picture your revelation is like having a car in your garage. It could be a million-dollar machine or a beaten-up old wreck worth very little. In reality, it is irrelevant what kind of car you have until you turn the key, leave the garage, and take it for a spin. Only then do you enjoy the quality of your vehicle. The quality of your car does not stop it from rusting and gathering dust in an empty and lifeless garage. Intimacy with God is the movement, the life, and the momentum that revelation facilitates.

Let me give one more example. Imagine if I took my wife, Christine, out to a beautiful restaurant. We've planned this hot date for a month and are hungry and excited to dine in style. We are ushered to our fancy table, seated with a breathtaking ocean view, and presented with the menu. We look around at what other people are eating, can smell the aroma of fine cuisine, and our mouths are watering as we anticipate our meal.

We pick up our menus and look through them, commenting on the fine-sounding food, the tasty-looking condiments, and the evident culinary creativity. As time goes by, we look in more and more detail at the menu. We comment on the font used to type the menu, the cardboard density, and the laminate. We even argue over what some confusing foreign words could mean, googling the meanings. We take photos of the menu to show our friends and quote lines from it on our social media pages.

After increasingly confusing the waitress for a couple of hours, because we have yet to order a meal and the evening is drawing to an end, we then stand up and leave the restaurant! We go home hungry, having been content to *look* at the menu but never order a meal from it.

Sounds like a nightmare, right? This is what it is like to never embrace intimacy with your revelation of God! This is how many Christians read the Scriptures. The Bible is intended to nourish our souls and propel us into a relationship with God. Its purpose is not to satisfy our intellect apart from intimacy! Never stare at the menu without ordering a meal!

RIGHTEOUSNESS IS THE DOOR

Your revelation of righteousness is like a door. When you open the door and go through it, you enter the bedroom, the place of intimacy with God. If you are not careful, you will stand at the door, study the door, teach about the door, even argue about the door, but never walk through it. Don't be known for how well you understand the truth or can discuss doctrine. Be known for knowing Him.

*A door may as well be a wall if you never
actually walk through it.*

The door of righteousness is extremely important. It gives us compatible access to the room of intimacy with God, but it is a door nonetheless. The value of the door is ultimately found in the room it gives us access to. Right standing with God and a nature like His is a priceless reality, but knowing it is just the beginning. *Enjoying it* is our inheritance.

We have no need in the church for a new "camp." We must not become yet another movement, this time known as "righteousness people." But we can finally become "Jesus people," because we have transcended every limiting identity and found ourselves perfectly in the person of God!

Righteousness is not the end goal; it is the entrance to intimacy.

This is why, if applied appropriately, righteousness will not just be another theological camp. It is an awakening to an incorruptible way of identifying ourselves, rooted in the reality of the Father alone. We will not bicker and backbite, defending our special doctrine. We will live in the fullness of intimacy with God and the power of His love that righteousness gives us access to.

I want to show you that the world is not looking for a new revelation or a powerful doctrine. It's seeking to know the Father—Christians and non-Christians alike.

*"He has put eternity into man's heart, yet so that he cannot find
out what God has done from the beginning to the end."*
ECCLESIASTES 3:11

Eternity is on every man's heart. Does that mean every man wants to live forever? No. Jesus told us what eternity is:

"And this is eternal life, that they know you the only true God, and Jesus Christ whom you have sent."

JOHN 17:3

Jesus taught us here that eternal life is not merely an endless span of time, it is an eternal relationship with God! Eternal life is that we might *know God*. Relationship with Him is the reason we are alive, *and* it is our never-ending destiny! God has placed this eternity in the heart of every man. This means the deepest desire of every human being is to know God. Unbelievers will humble themselves, repent, and receive Jesus when we walk in an undeniable intimacy with God—not when we parade our doctrines.

I am making no effort to devalue revelation here. That would mean devaluing this entire book. What I am doing is exalting relationship with God as the ultimate *reason* for revelation.

THE CORE OF THE COVENANT

When God describes the very heart of the new covenant, we see His purpose is a relationship. It is a covenant of intimacy of Him in you and you in Him. Look at what He has to say about His desire for you, revealed by the new covenant you live in:

"For this is the covenant that I will make with the house of Israel, after those days, declares the Lord: I will put my laws into their minds, and write them on their hearts, and I will be their God, and they shall be my people. And they shall not teach, each one his neighbor and each one his brother, saying, 'Know the Lord,' for they shall all know me, from the least of them to the greatest. For I will be merciful toward their iniquities, and I will remember their sins no more."

HEBREWS 8:10-12

All will know Him. Intimacy, relationship, and love: these are at the heart of the new covenant. The reason all will know Him is because He will "be merciful toward their [our] iniquities and remember their [our] sins no more." This is righteousness: the removal of our sins and the gift of our right standing with God. Righteousness is the reason we can know the Father. Righteousness is the door to the place of intimacy with God. But intimacy with God is the reason for righteousness, the reason you and I breathe and the purpose we were created for.

The declaration of God to you is: *I created you to know me, to be loved by me, to be like me.* You and I walked away from Him, making ourselves incompatible with Him when we took on a sinful nature in Adam. He restored our compatibility on the cross.

The most astounding statement of the incarnation of Jesus is this: *God fits in man.* He made us so He could live in us. God desires a relationship with us more than the devil would have us know. He is not a distant and mildly displeased God. He is a Father who has crossed the time and space sin put between us, taken the sinful nature out of us in every way, and restored us to a perfect union with Him in the Godhead. We now know God has placed a desire for a relationship with Him on our hearts. We also know He deeply desires a relationship with us. The only thing left to do is to get the necessary understanding and embrace this incredible love relationship.

The enemy is more frightened of you knowing the Father than of anything else. Guilt, shame, condemnation, and the reminders of your past are his attempts to keep you from pursuing intimacy with God.

Remember, God remembers the sins of your past no more, so how could He ever be the one bringing them up? The cross declares you are worth the blood of God Himself. The cross declares your forgiveness. You are of the highest value to the Father. He could have destroyed humanity after our Adamic fall. He could have started over. But He saw you from before the beginning. He saw that you would believe in Him and pursue the relationship He created you to have. He decided you were worth all the pain, loss, and destruction that would result from the fall. He would at least get *you*. He loves you more than you can ever truly know.

Please stop for a minute and take a moment to take what you have found here to the Father. Dialogue this powerful revelation of righteousness with Him. Do not just study about Him, or about your new life in Him. He is in the room with you, yearning for you. He desires *you*.

> *Both the purpose of revelation and the origin of revelation is intimacy with God.*

May this generation be one of intimacy. May people of righteousness be known above all else for their deep relationship with God. May we move far beyond the sinner saved by grace paradigm and boldly walk in the fiery and secure fellowship of God Himself, seeing entire nations awake to His love and purpose. We are this generation.

PART THREE
CRITICAL CLARITY

CHAPTER 11

JESUS, THE WILL AND NATURE OF GOD REVEALED

"Jesus Christ alone can reveal the Father."
CHARLES H. SPURGEON[1]

I found a Christian tract in my mailbox once. I had been a Christian for years when I read it, but was only now was I having my world shaken by what the Scriptures taught about the Father's heart toward us. The kindness, jealousy, and perseverance He had shown in aiming to win our hearts back to Him was breathtaking. Jesus was drawing *all* men to Himself (John 12:32).

I stood there at the mailbox stunned. "If you do not read this tract, you have no integrity" it began. Something like, "God hates you because of your sin" followed. It got worse as I read on. Previously in my Christian life, I would not have thought much about this, but not now. Now I had tasted that the Lord was good (1 Peter 2:3). God had ravished my heart with His eternal love, delivered me from demonic oppression and addiction, and made me whole. I deeply knew of His kindness and love that had led me to repentance (Romans 2:4). I could not conceive of this tract doing anything but pushing people further from the Father. It drastically misrepresented Him.

A statement raced through my mind loudly: *All the world needs is to see me as I really am.* If we see the Father as He really is—with His goodness, love, redemption, and nearness—everything changes. I was flooded with the realization that many Christians did not know the Father, myself included, for many years.

I ran into my house and threw myself on the bed, sobbing so much my bed was wet with tears. In those moments, His love, kindness, and true nature were overwhelming me. He was showing me His goodness, His intentions, our eternal significance to the Father as His children, and our general blindness to it all.

It has occurred to me since that the goodness of God, His true nature, and His desires have been challenged all the way back to the garden of Eden. When the enemy questioned the validity and trustworthiness of God's words to Adam and Eve, he was challenging God's goodness. This is why the apostle John—the "apostle of love," as many have named him—the apostle closest to the heart of Jesus and who had grasped the revelation of Christ so profoundly, could write:

> *"This is the message we have heard from him and proclaim to you, that God is light, and in him is no darkness at all."*
> **1 JOHN 1:5**

John the Baptist summed up Jesus's *mission* in a sentence (John 1:29).

The apostle John summed up Jesus's *message,* the fundamental declaration of the incarnated God, in a sentence: "God is light!" Why was this Jesus's message to humanity? Why not something about hell or heaven, communion or baptism, divine healing or eschatology? Because none of these things can rightly be understood apart from intimate knowledge of the eternal *goodness* of God. This is precisely the thing the devil has spent thousands of years trying to pervert, stain, and deceive us about.

The devil hates the goodness of God. This is because God's goodness

- leads us to repentance (Romans 2:4),

- leads us into a relationship,

- makes us whole,

- helps us grow into our salvation and Christian character (1 Peter 2:2–3),

- fills us with hope,

- helps us trust Him, and

- helps us feel safe to engage with Him.

It changes *everything.* Jesus came to change our minds from the way we had grown to see the Father: through a twisted, fallen lens (Colossians 1:21). He came to restore the reputation of the Godhead while ridding us of the sinful nature that had put us at enmity with Him. We had been viewing God through a veil of deception, wrongly interpreting Him through the shadows of the old covenant, making flawed conclusions about His nature, intentions, and desires (2 Corinthians 3:14–15). Sadly, many still are.

I was overcome by jealousy for the Lord's reputation that day. I leaped off my tear-soaked bed and marched up and down the streets in my neighborhood, pulling all the tracts out of people's mailboxes. I had never really evangelized, apart from rare moments of pressure and compulsion, but now a burning desire for people to know the goodness and love of God drove me, as it has ever since. If I did not see the tract in a particular mailbox, I would knock on the door of the person's home, still crying, explaining to him God truly loved him and to please ignore the message of the tract he'd received. I did this for a couple of hours before returning home to phone the church that had published the tract. I cried more on the phone and begged them to stop misrepresenting the heart of God. They told me I should pay them for the printing costs I had wasted in throwing all their tracts out!

I might not react the same way today. I had serious zeal but little wisdom. However, I am as zealous as ever about restoring God's reputation to humanity so that *all* will see Him and know Him as He is—inside and outside the church.

THE SHADOWS AND THE SUBSTANCE

"The New is in the Old concealed, the Old is in the New revealed."
ST. AUGUSTINE[2]

Imagine getting a phone call one day from a radio competition hotline. They excitedly tell you that you are live on the air with them *right now*. They then announce you are the winner of the grand prize in a competition they are running! You remember you entered a competition at a shopping center kiosk recently. "Would you like to know what your prize is?" they ask. "Yes," you reply excitedly.

The next thing they say shocks you. They shout through the phone, "You have won a meal with Adolf Hitler!" Your heart skips a beat. Fear grips you. *What? Why would I want to spend the night with him?* you think to yourself. The company then gives you a phone number to call when you are ready to redeem your prize and hang up the phone. You have just been given complete access to the presence of Hitler, anytime you want. You are entitled to it and completely qualified to meet with him. Do you think you will call the number and redeem your prize? Of course not!

Sadly, because of serious misunderstandings, many have failed to see the Father as He really is. We have been given access to a God we sometimes feel is as unpredictable and unapproachable as Hitler was. Righteousness is the door to intimacy with the Father. Even though you'll learn through this book that we have perfect access to the Father, many will still not enter the door after reading it until they change their minds about who the Father is.

If we do not redeem the goodness of God in our generation, we will develop the language of righteousness but remain afraid of having intimacy with God.

This would be an absolute disaster, making us walking contradictions. Imagine knowing and teaching a message that oozes with access to the intimate presence of God, but having no evidence of that intimacy in our own lives. It would devalue, and create disdain toward, the message of righteousness. We are alive to know Him, not to know the doctrine of "the door" and stop there. Our revelation is only as good as the intimacy it produces. A door may as well be a wall if we never walk through it.

A huge reason for our misunderstanding of the Father comes from wrongly interpreting Scripture, or missing what Jesus revealed about the Father in His life. If what we think about God is not expressed in the person of Jesus and His earthly life, then we are probably misunderstanding God. If we interpret who the Father is by our experiences, our traditions, or even from the Old Testament alone, without the insight of Christ's life, then we are probably wrongly informed about the nature of God.

Look at how these verses speak of the Old Testament and how they served as a shadow of what was to come:

"These are a shadow of the things to come, but the substance belongs to Christ."
COLOSSIANS 2:17

"They serve a copy and shadow of the heavenly things. For when Moses was about to erect the tent, he was instructed by God, saying, "See that you make everything according to the pattern that was shown you on the mountain."
HEBREWS 8:5

"For just as Jonah was three days and three nights in the belly of the great fish, so will the Son of Man be three days and three nights in the heart of the earth."
MATTHEW 12:40

(This is one example of many where Jesus referred to Old Testament passages as a type and shadow of Himself.)

"You search the Scriptures because you think that in them you have eternal life; and it is they that bear witness about me, yet you refuse to come to me that you may have life."
JOHN 5:39-40

Jesus is the substance of what was shadowed in the Old Testament.

Often we make the mistake of determining God's will or nature by His actions recorded in the Old Testament, under the old covenant. God's will and nature cannot be determined apart from seeing Him in Christ and through the new covenant, which was His ultimate plan for us. The

Old Testament can then beautifully reinforce the dynamics of His nature we find in the New Testament, showing us what was really going on and how the covenants of old were affecting man's walk with God. If we mistake the shadow for the substance, we will misunderstand who God is and what He does on the earth today. We may even attribute responsibility of things resembling old covenant judgment in the world today to Him by citing things such as earthquakes, tsunamis, wildfires, wars, and more.

We must not imagine God is still relating to us under His old covenant with man. The new covenant has come, allowing the relationship He always desired to have with us. He has led us on a journey of covenants to help us discover our need for a savior from our sin—bringing us into His eternal desire: into the new covenant of freedom and fellowship with Him. In the new covenant, Jesus came to bring a new agreement with man to light: "life and life in abundance" (John 10:10).

Fantastic evidence of this is found in Luke 9. Look at how Jesus revealed the truth about God's intentions when His disciples tried to act the way they thought God wanted them to, based on their old covenant understanding. Jesus was rejected by a Samaritan village on His way to Jerusalem. John and James witnessed this rejection, so filled with indignation at how they'd treated "their" Jesus, they approached Jesus and asked, "Lord, do You want us to command fire to come down from heaven and consume them, just as Elijah did?" (Luke 9:54).

Although the disciples were catching on that Jesus was the Messiah, and He represented God, they still had the echo of Old Testament destruction and judgment in their understanding of God. Of course, this is what they expected Jesus would want them to do. However, Jesus, now modeling the new covenant, replied with a startling change of insight about God's will and nature. "He turned and rebuked them, and said, 'You do not know what manner of spirit you are of. For the Son of Man did not come to destroy men's lives but to save them'" (Luke 9:55–56). Wow! John and

James were mimicking what they understood of God in His old covenant relations to man. Jesus, however, who ultimately revealed the will and nature of God, presented a correction that changed everything about the ways they thought God functioned.

> *We can only interpret the shadows of the Old Testament through the explicit message of the New Testament.*

Jesus revealed perfectly who the Father is. Jesus revealed the nature of the entire Godhead and God's ultimate, transcendent desires for humanity. We cannot learn much about someone from studying his shadow! We must study the substance and then rightly discern the shadows.

IF YOU CAN'T SEE IT IN THE SON, DON'T CALL IT THE FATHER!

All Christian theology must be rooted in the life and message of Jesus. He is the truth about God, period. Does Job reveal the clearest truth about God? No, Jesus does. Does the book of Exodus reveal the unveiled will of God? No, Jesus does. We can only rightly understand the Old Testament through the New Testament. Once we learn the purpose, will, and nature of God in Jesus, we can discern God's ways and wisdom in the book of Job and Exodus, seeing clear evidence of His nature and rightly discerning the message of these books, but not apart from the insight of Christ's life. We can only rightly understand God through Jesus when the mystery is finally revealed and the veil is removed—through which we were relating to God. Let's look at some Bible verses on this:

> *"No one has ever seen God; the only God, who is at the Father's side, He (Jesus) has made Him known."*
>
> **JOHN 1:18**

Jesus makes the unseen God visible and known. He is the truth about God.

"If you had known me, you would have known my Father also.
From now on you do know Him and have seen Him." Philip
said to him, "Lord, show us the Father, and it is enough for
us." Jesus said to him, "Have I been with you so long, and you
still do not know me, Philip? Whoever has seen me has seen the
Father. How can you say, 'Show us the Father?'"

JOHN 14:7–9

Jesus was in such oneness and cohesion with the Father He could say this. To know Jesus *is* also to know the Father. To see Him is to see the Father.

"He (Jesus) is the image of the invisible God, the
firstborn of all creation."

COLOSSIANS 1:15

"Long ago, at many times and in many ways, God spoke to our
fathers by the prophets, but in these last days He has spoken
to us by His Son, whom He appointed the heir of all things,
through whom also he created the world. He is the radiance of
the glory of God and the exact imprint of His nature, and He
upholds the universe by the word of His power. After making
purification for sins, He sat down at the right hand of the
Majesty on high."

HEBREWS 1:1-3

Jesus is the final word about the nature and heart of the Godhead. He is the exact imprint of God's nature. He is the perfect representation of the Father—not just a portion of the Father either. The entire Godhead is revealed in Christ. Jesus even made the offensive statement to the Jews, "No one knows the Father except the Son" (Luke 10:22; Matthew 11:27). After thousands of years of relating to God as they thought He was, according to what they believed He wanted, and veiled to His true desires by the old covenant, Jesus told them they were wrong about God.

Does He also have the ultimate authority on the will of God? Let's see:

"Making known to us the mystery of His will, according to His purpose, which He set forth in Christ."

EPHESIANS 1:9

"So Jesus said to them, "Truly, truly, I say to you, the Son can do nothing of His own accord, but only what He sees the Father doing. For whatever the Father does, that the Son does likewise."

JOHN 5:19

The author of Hebrews quoted Psalm 40 as Christ speaking to the Father saying:

"Sacrifices and offerings you have not desired, but a body have you prepared for me; in burnt offerings and sin offerings you have taken no pleasure. Then I said, 'Behold, I have come to do your will, O God, as it is written of me in the scroll of the book.'"

HEBREWS 10:5-7

Jesus declared He alone revealed and fulfilled the will of God. He showed we had been wrong about God, but He declared and revealed Him to us, finally removing the veil the old covenant put over our eyes toward God (2 Corinthians 3:14–15).

This is extremely significant. Once you grasp this, you can never call something you experience the will of God or an act of God, if it is inconsistent with the things Jesus's life revealed about God. That makes things very narrow, and as a result, very safe. In the new covenant, *if you cannot see it in the Son, don't call it the Father.* Jesus is the perfect and exact representation of God. Jesus is not a separate and solitary person of the Godhead; He is filled with the entire Godhead! He represents the heart of the Trinity. Look at these verses:

"For in him the whole fullness of deity dwells bodily."
COLOSSIANS 2:9

This means all the Trinity takes up residence in the Son. Not just the "nice part" of the Father, but the Father. If you want to know who God is as a triune God, then look at Jesus!

"That is, in Christ God was reconciling the world to himself."
2 CORINTHIANS 5:19

The Father was in the Son, destroying sin in the flesh so He could reconcile the world to Himself. This was a triune effort, not a separate mission of the Son.

"I and the Father are one."
JOHN 10:30

We often draw wrong conclusions from God's actions under the old covenant—which He established to lead us into His eternally-desired new covenant. Due to these conclusions, our ideas about God's heart are misguided, and we have sometimes dissected the Trinity beyond what Scripture allows. By the time Jesus showed up, he seemed entirely different than the Father. We subtly concluded from our reading that the Father was a distant, displeased deity from the old covenant, and the Son was the more relatable member of the Trinity. Jesus modeled the new covenant relationship the entire Godhead desired to have with us, and He made it possible at the cross by ending the limited relationship of the old covenant. The Father is not still acting according to the old covenant while Jesus alone relates to us through the new covenant. The Father, the Son, and Holy Spirit now relate to us entirely under the new covenant.

The Bible says Jesus came to His own, but they did not know Him (John 1:10–11). I pray this would never be said of man again. The Trinity shares one nature. There is no dark, hidden corner of the Father that Jesus could not show us. He perfectly revealed who the Father was and is. When you rightly define the Father by what the Son revealed about Him, you can finally trust and know who God is, making it perfectly safe to go through the righteousness door into intimacy with your Father!

Some powerful implications of this are:

- If you decide God does not desire to heal the sick, restore the brokenhearted, and liberate the captives, then you must prove this through the Son. He healed all who came to Him (Matthew 4:23–34; 9:35; Luke 4:40–44; 6:17–19; 9:11).

- If you decide God wants to use evil, sickness, devastation, or poverty to teach or judge you, then you must prove this through the Son. Jesus came to do good and "destroy the works of the devil" (1 John 3:8), He came "not to destroy people's lives, but to save them" (Acts 10:38; John 3:17; 1 John 3:8; Luke 9:56).

- If you think God is judging nations for various laws passed, or for socially agreed upon sin, then you must prove this through the Son. He came to redeem us from our sin by revealing the love and goodness of God in Christ, not holding our trespasses against us (2 Corinthians 5:19). There is certainly a future day of judgment (Matthew 25:31–33; 1 Corinthians 4:5), but now is not that day.

- If you have seen the Son, then you have seen the Father (John 14:9). This is final. It doesn't say you have seen some aspects of the Father.

- Seeing Jesus shows us everything we need to know about the Father. Nothing about the Father is hidden from us (John 1:18; Colossians 1:15; Hebrews 1:1–3).

- Jesus only did and said what He saw the Father doing and saying (John 5:19; 12:49). If Jesus did not say or do it, neither does the Father!

- Jesus represented the entire Godhead, not just the Son

independently (Colossians 2:9; 1:15; John 1:18).

If your theology of God is inconsistent with the life of Jesus, then you need to rethink your theology about God. If we continue to believe the Father is as drastically different from the Son as we have done in the church, we are departing from monotheism and verging on polytheism. This makes the Trinity three different gods, with three different natures and desires. This is a departure from Christianity. The Trinity shares the same heart, nature, desires, and intentions for creation. They can be distinguished from one another but *never* separated. Jesus is the only true and tangible revelation of the Godhead. God really is good. The apostle John meant it when he said there was *no darkness* in God, and Jesus proved it to us. It is critical you decide in your heart that in the face of any attack or suggestion of the enemy—no matter what comes your way in life—if it does not look like the Son, you will never call it the Father.

A statement I use frequently, which has become a foundational statement to all I teach, is this:

Jesus Christ is the truth about God and the truth about us.

If you can remember this statement, and explore it with Holy Spirit in the Scriptures, you will know God accurately and rightly know yourself in Him.

THE SOVEREIGNTY OF GOD

This brings me to sovereignty, which possibly has crossed some minds during this chapter. Some serious clarity needs to be brought. I cannot address the issue fully here, as multiple other thoughts are linked to sovereignty, such as predestination and election. I also do not have all the answers, but I pray that some would begin seeking a fresh scriptural understanding as a result of the following conclusions. The Bible paints a very different picture of God's sovereignty than our modern Christian culture sometimes does. Some call it sovereignty, selection, or "God allowing." When it is said, people often are implying that every single thing that takes place on our planet and in our lives is God's administrative decision for us; that He is in perfect transcendent and total control over every detail of the cosmos, enacting and governing every event of our lives.

If you are sick, it is God. If a city is destroyed, also God. If you lose your job, God. If you get a job, God. Everything is God. We are made to sing songs about His goodness, yet we are deeply confused about Him in our hearts because something terrible happened: like our loved one died, and our theology dictates God took him. Even multiple non-Christians I have offered prayer to have a subtle idea in their minds that God caused their sickness in the first place, believing God causes everything. I believe the enemy plants this belief in people to keep them from the Father (1 Peter 5:8; John 8:44). As the Father's representatives on the earth, we must not reinforce this lie. Because of this teaching, some have made God out to be like an emperor, giving a thumbs-up or thumbs-down on every detail of our lives, good and bad. The theological term for this flawed understanding is often termed "sovereignty," but is more accurately called "absolute sovereignty." We will see God is certainly sovereign, but not "absolutely sovereign" in the way I have described above.

The problems with absolute sovereignty are significant. First, it is unscriptural when compared to the revelation of Christ. Second, it can make God out to be an abusive, manipulative, unpredictable God. Happy one day, furious the next. Literally as fickle as the weather, like a dictator. This is because instead of using the life of Jesus as our perspective of God, our belief in sovereignty limits us to determining what His "hidden" or sovereign will is by what happens to us in our day-to-day lives. It makes us comfortable to think God the Father is nothing like God the Son, but that contradicts everything we just looked at about what Jesus represents. We must not take tricky passages of Scripture like Romans 9, where some of this thinking originates, and interpret them apart from the type of Christocentric theology observed here, drawing conclusions that do not keep to Christ's revelation of the Father, or a proper division of the covenants at the centre of our understanding.

> *You cannot be a representative for someone*
> *whose heart you do not know*

Picture a father who tells his young son not to put his hand on the burner. The father takes precautions and teaches the son why he should not do it. The son then disobeys the father, touches the burner, and burns his hand. The father rushes to his aid, holds him, nurses him, and then teaches him the pain is what he was trying to prevent. This is healthy parenting. The absolute sovereignty of God doctrine applied to this scenario makes the father out to be the careful planner of the accident, orchestrating the son's hand touching the burner to burn his hand so he can then teach the son something through the pain. In the world we would call this child abuse, but many are comfortable with viewing God this way and labelling it sovereignty.

John Calvin was pivotal in pioneering modern language for this way of thinking, drawing conclusions like "For what seems more attributable to chance than the branch which falls from a tree, and kills the passing traveler? But the Lord sees very differently, and declares that He delivered him into the hand of the slayer," and "God, Who enlightens all, has his own eye always open, and thus exhorts the poor to patient endurance, seeing that those who are discontented with their lot endeavor to shake off a burden which God has imposed upon them."[3]

Where the word sovereign is used in some translations, it is always used in association with the word "Lord" and is the same as the King James Version's

"Lord God." Not a single time is the word "sovereign" used in the manner used in some circles today. Is God sovereign? Yes. God is sovereign in the sense He is supreme. There is no one higher in authority or strength; He can also act apart from us, doing great works on the earth in His power, as we invite Him in prayer and partner with His will on the earth (Acts 4:29–31). But that does not mean He exercises His power by controlling everything in our lives, nor does it mean He functions outside of His good nature, revealed in the life of His Son. If God were to violate what He has revealed about Himself in His son, He would undermine His integrity and trustworthiness, which He will never do (Psalms 138:2). He revealed His will in Christ, period.

The belief in "absolute sovereignty" sometimes goes to such a devastating degree that God is ultimately the one to blame for the devil's works, which completely ignores the involvement of the enemy and the decisions of our human will. This belief can make Christians passive toward overcoming the enemy; they leave their God-given authority and power to lie dormant and act as if their hands are tied.

Here are several truths that bring serious question to this flawed way of thinking about God's absolute sovereignty:

- The kingdom of God is at hand and He has given us the keys. We must not blame everything on a wrong idea of God's sovereignty when we should use the authority given to us to establish His purpose (Luke 10:19; Matthew 16:19).

- God wills that none should perish, but that all would come to the knowledge of the truth and be saved (2 Peter 3:9; 1 Timothy 2:4). This is a clear example of His desire and purpose. Are people dying and going to hell every day? Yes. Is it God's will they would be saved instead? Yes. If God's will is absolutely sovereign, then we have a serious problem here. It is not God's will that's sending people to hell.

- If everything is God, then why do we have a sword/shield and power/authority (Ephesians 6:10–18; Luke 10:17; Matthew 28:18–20)? What are we using these weapons to fight against? God's sovereign plan?

- If everything is God, then why did He tell us to bind and loose according to heaven's design on the earth (Matthew 16:18–19)?

- If everything is God, then why has He given the earth to the sons of men (Psalms 115:16)?

- If everything is God, why do we have the power of life and death in our tongues (Proverbs 18:21)?

- If everything is God, why do you reap what you sow (Galatians 6:8)?

- If everything is God, then why are people destroyed for lack of knowledge (Hosea 4:6)? Some conclude destruction is the will of God, but the Bible calls it lack of knowledge.

- If everything is God, then why speak to the mountain? If God wants it moved, then He will move it! (Matthew 17:20; Mark 11:23).

- If everything is God, then why even go to the hospital to be healed? You are fighting God's sovereign order.

- Why make any requests of God for safety, provision, weather, healing, wholeness, or people to be saved?

- If everything is God, then why did Jesus say if we abide in His Word we would know the truth, and the truth would set us free (John 8:31–32)? Perhaps we need the truth to set us free. Our brokenness is not His sovereign plan.

- If God the Father was sovereignly responsible for all the sick people in the Gospels, then why was God the Son healing them all? This would make God completely at odds with Himself (Acts 10:38; 1 John 3:8).

*"O Jerusalem, Jerusalem, the city that kills the prophets
and stones those who are sent to it! How often would I have
gathered your children together as a hen gathers her brood
under her wings, and you were not willing!"*
MATTHEW 23:37

Here, Jesus had a strong desire for His people, but because the will of the people differed from His, He could not fulfill His desire.

God has taken the earth and given it to His children to steward (Psalms 115:16). We are now *co-laboring* with Him, in His will, destroying the works of darkness with Him as His royal priesthood (1 Peter 2:9). For too long we have labeled the will of God a mystery, but the Bible says we are foolish if we do not know His will once Christ reveals it (Ephesians 5:17)! His will has clearly been revealed so we can faithfully manifest it on the earth as His empowered representatives.

The unbalanced idea of absolute sovereignty is a devastating idea. It leaves Christians powerless when their loved ones go through torment, sickness, and pain, believing it is God's will, ultimately making God responsible for the works of the devil. It must leave our thinking. Jesus said in John 14:12 that anyone who believes in Him will do the works He did, which means we should destroy the works of the devil too, not uphold a false understanding of sovereignty and succumb to helplessness.

It is time we stop blaming Him and start believing Him.

In the new covenant, God is not ordaining disaster in your life, giving your loved ones cancer, or creating your challenging circumstance to teach you a lesson. He will turn all things for good for those who love Him, and father us through every challenge we face, but that in no way declares He is *causing* all things (Romans 8:28). Some suggest that God is still causing

JESUS, THE WILL AND NATURE OF GOD REVEALED

suffering on the earth today, because He ultimately caused the suffering of His son. But this suffering was so that we would be delivered from the curse of sin, death, and the law and be enabled to live in a new covenant, which is a covenant of abundant life, mercy, and sonship, revealed clearly in Jesus's life (John 10:10; Acts 10:38; Matt 28:18–20; Luke 9:1;10:1; Matthew 10:1; Galatians 3:13; Romans 8:1). His chastisement on our behalf purchased our *peace*, it was not an example or an explanation for suffering in our lives (Isaiah 53:5). I have seen the mindset of absolute sovereignty damage entire families, crush hope, and rob people's trust in the Father.

Having this misguided view of sovereignty makes God more like a yin and yang God (both dark and light). It makes Him unpredictable and untrustworthy. Despite John summing up Jesus's entire message in one sentence, declaring He is perfect light, we have created a theological loophole where we can pin darkness on God while still calling Him good.

There are a few verses in which the word "sovereign" is used (Acts 4:24; 1 Timothy 6:15; Revelation 6:10). The Greek terms mean God is "absolute Lord or master," or a person of "great authority."[4] This is nothing like what many have made it out to be. Simply put, by creating humans with a will, God chose not to take total control. Love that cannot be chosen, is not ultimately love. It's much like a president can be in charge but not ultimately in control of the citizens in the nation he governs. He can lead benevolently, create laws that benefit society, and even put law enforcement in place to keep things on track. But if someone violently shoots someone else on the street, the president is not personally in control of this, neither did he desire or even allow it. In the kingdom, the church is empowered to be God's law enforcement against the influence of darkness. We must pursue a correct understanding of our mission and take responsibility for it.

Often it is our wrong decisions or an attack from the devil that brings disaster upon us. Sometimes the natural results of a fallen world cause us pain. Our tragedies are not the cause, nor the judgment of God, and God's omnipresence in no way dictates His total control over these things. James clearly taught that God is responsible for "every good gift and perfect gift" that comes down from above, from the "Father of Lights" (James 1:17). This draws quite a line in the sand.

> *"I call heaven and earth to witness against you today, that I*
> *have set before you life and death, blessing and curse. Therefore*
> *choose life, that you and your offspring may live."*
> **DEUTERONOMY 30:19**

God has a plan for every person's life (Jeremiah 29:11), but He doesn't make us walk that path, and the specifics of His plans are usually far more diverse and spacious than we realize. He has presented life and death before us, and as a loving Father, He is compelling us to choose life. He is not choosing death or life for us based only on how our circumstances go. We have the ability to choose. God cannot force us to choose Him; He can only present life to us in His Son for all men to see, inviting us into His loving arms of redemption and eternal life.

The same message the apostle John declared to us is now our message to declare to the world:

> *"God is light; there is no darkness in Him."*
> **1 JOHN 1:5**

Let's be people who know the goodness of God rather than people who are confused about the Father. Let's be confident in Christ's perfect revelation of His ways, His will, and His nature.

(ENDNOTES)

1. Charles H. Spurgeon, *Spurgeon's Sermons on Prayer p.468*
2. Warren W. Wiersbe, *Wiersbe Bible Commentary 2 Vol Set* w/CD Rom (Wiersbe Bible Commentaries) (Colorado Springs: David C. Cook; New edition, 2007).
3. Christian History Institute. "Calvin on God's Sovereignty." Dan Graves, ed. www.christianhistoryinstitute.org/study/module/calvin-on-gods-sovereignty.
4. *Strong's* G1413

CHAPTER 12
GRACE

Grace is the key that holds righteousness together. It is the ingredient that replaces any works-based effort to manifest our new nature and produces a far more powerful and authentic holiness. Look at how grace and righteousness are a combo for reigning in life in the verses below. Without grace, enabled by Holy Spirit, we would be stuck with nothing but our effort to make our new righteous nature function. Let's look at this reality in Scripture.

> *"For if, because of one man's trespass, death reigned through*
> *that one man, much more will those who receive the abundance*
> *of grace and the free gift of righteousness reign in life through*
> *the one man Jesus Christ."*
> **ROMANS 5:17**

"So that, as sin reigned in death, grace also might reign through righteousness leading to eternal life through Jesus Christ our Lord."
ROMANS 5:21

Grace and righteousness working together is what enables us to reign in life. Many are blowing a grace trumpet these days. Many have blown a righteousness trumpet too. Without a real understanding of both, though, and without an overarching emphasis on intimacy with God, we cannot have the full, well-rounded picture. Without knowing the truth about grace *and* righteousness, we will see an unhealthy emphasis of each in different "camps." One can create self-righteous works; the other can create a "grace complacency."

We understand a measure of what grace *is*, but apart from rightly defining ourselves as righteous, we cannot properly know what grace *does*. We must discover the righteousness grace is supposed to reign through.

You can see in the above verses that grace reigns *through* righteousness, not apart from it. We now know righteousness is not a distant promise of a new nature but a fully given gift of God already living inside us. It is our new holy nature, completely replacing the old, sinful nature when we get born again. It results from God's divine nature we partook of when we received Jesus (2 Peter 1:3). We died with Jesus and took on His righteous nature as our own (2 Corinthians 5:21; Romans 6:6; Galatians 2:20; Colossians 3:3; 2 Peter 1:3). With this in mind, we will focus largely on what grace is and how it works in partnership with our new righteous nature.

When we rightly understand these two powerful truths, our lives can be utterly transformed through intimacy with God and by faith. Let's examine how this works. Please prayerfully consider the following verses, as they are a powerful key to a transformed life.

WHAT ON EARTH IS GRACE?

*"Nothing whatever in the way of goodness pertaining to godliness
and real holiness can be accomplished without it [grace]."*
ST. AUGUSTINE, THE CONFESSIONS OF ST. AUGUSTINE[1]

Grace is not a covering for a sinful condition we retain from the Adamic fall
once we enter into Christ. The "sinner saved by grace" misinterpretation
is rapidly diminishing across the globe, and the "covering" interpretation
of grace is no longer a fitting description. Once we understand our new
righteous nature, we must reinterpret grace.

To label grace as "unmerited favor" is absolutely accurate. The fact God has
redeemed us apart from anything we can do to deserve or earn His favor is
an overwhelming truth. We should meditate on and revel in this profound
reality always. However, this description falls far short of what grace truly
is or what it can do. Let's examine a few Scriptures:

*"For the grace of God has appeared, bringing salvation for
all people, training us to renounce ungodliness and worldly
passions, and to live self-controlled, upright, and godly lives in
the present age."*
TITUS 2:11-12

First, grace is displayed in the person of Christ, bringing salvation for
us. Unmerited favor makes us righteous. We read on to see grace is also
the inner enabling of God's divine nature that trains us and functions
within us, causing the life of God to pour out of us. Grace is God's
continuing work in our inner man and our salvation. Grace is the reality
that compels us to put off sin and to live holy lives. It causes the fruit of
our righteousness to manifest as we believe the truth.

"But by the grace of God I am what I am, and his grace toward
me was not in vain. On the contrary, I worked harder than any of
them, though it was not I, but the grace of God that is with me."
1 CORINTHIANS 15:10

This is huge. Grace is the enablement that caused Paul to accomplish what he *did* and determined who he *was*. Grace was the empowering force behind his entire life, ministry, holiness, and persistence in preaching the gospel. Our job is to reckon ourselves dead to sin and alive to God through Christ Jesus (Romans 6:11), so that by recognizing the truth, the indwelling and ongoing grace of God can empower this reality in our lives. We are not only saved by grace but empowered in life by grace too!

"You then, my child, be strengthened by the grace that is
in Christ Jesus."
2 TIMOTHY 2:1

Grace is in Christ, as are we. It is a new way of life in the new covenant. It is something we become strong in by revelation and intimacy with God; it works apart from human effort and is issued from our union with Jesus. Grace is the divine enablement of God in us—not a separate ambiguous element of our nature, but an attribute of His. Some suggest grace is, in fact, Jesus, or a person, and that when Paul said, "The grace of God has appeared" (Titus 2:11), this referred to Jesus. In the same way sin can be a personified extension of the enemy; grace is a personified extension of Christ. Some suggest perhaps Holy Spirit is grace personified, as some interesting verses imply, for example:

Then he said to me, "This is the word of the Lord to
Zerubbabel: Not by might, nor by power, but by my Spirit,
says the Lord of hosts. Who are you, O great mountain? Before
Zerubbabel you shall become a plain. And he shall bring
forward the top stone amid shouts of 'Grace, grace to it!'"
ZECHARIAH 4:6-7

It seems grace is too distinguishable from the person of Christ and Holy Spirit for them to conclusively be grace "personified" in Scripture. However, what grace does and what God does within us are very difficult to separate (also Hebrews 4:16; 10:29). It is probably needless to separate them anyway. Avoiding a strong separation aids us in seeing grace in a relational way regarding God's working of grace within us, rather than as a mere doctrine to have a cognitive agreement with. Instead of arguing for or against personified grace, I wish primarily to show that grace is an enabling reality within us, empowered by God, and not just unmerited favor.

We see more evidence of indwelling grace in our lives when we step into situations we need it for. Then we rest in God's grace to give us the answers and actions we need. Suddenly, we are achieving great exploits for His kingdom, and it is all enabled by the grace God endows us with to do it. His job is to give us the grace; our job is to get the understanding and walk in the truth. Grace then enables the truth to become our reality in any situation.

Mounce's Complete Expository Dictionary defines grace in a variety of ways, including this: "Grace is a new domain in which and by which Christians live (Romans 15:15, 16, 20). In this realm sin no longer rules (6:14). By His grace, God affects Christians' personal lives, giving them the ability to obey the gospel from the heart (Romans 6:17)!"[2] What a beautiful description. So grace is unmerited favor, but it's also an enabling attribute of our union with Christ.

WHEN AND HOW DO YOU GET GRACE?

When do you receive this grace that empowers you to live transformed? You receive it when you are born again. You do not have to get more grace, earn grace (an oxymoron), or exchange faith for grace. He gave you abundant grace in Christ.

"For from his fullness we have all received, grace upon grace."
JOHN 1:16

You are filled with grace when you are converted. God makes you a new creation by grace and then sets out to cause your new creation life to manifest when you walk in the belief of who you now are. Here are more verses claiming your grace-filled state:

"I give thanks to my God always for you because of the grace of God that was given you in Christ Jesus."
1 CORINTHIANS 1:4

"Through Him we have also obtained access by faith into this grace in which we stand, and we rejoice in hope of the glory of God."
ROMANS 5:2

"In Him we have redemption through His blood, the forgiveness of our trespasses, according to the riches of his grace, which he lavished upon us, in all wisdom and insight."
EPHESIANS 1:7-8

He lavished His grace upon us! The Greek word here is *perisseuō* and means "to super abound" or "above the needed measure with left over to spare!"[3] You do not need more grace. In Christ, you have more than you will ever be able to use. He has furnished you richly and affluently with grace to empower your Christian walk.

THE ACTIVE INGREDIENT

My good friend David Ridley, leader of our church in Darwin and an influential minister, calls grace the "active ingredient" of the Christian life—the thing that makes it work.

The apostle Paul knew God's grace was His divine influence upon our old nature that recreated us into His image and likeness again as new creations. He also discovered grace then behaves like the active ingredient in our new lives, functioning as Holy Spirit works it in our inner man. Like an electrical current, grace makes the new righteous wiring system in our inner walls live! God gives us a new electrical circuit and then flips the switch so grace can empower us as we believe the reality of what He accomplished.

Strong's Concordance says grace is: "the divine influence upon the heart, and its reflection in the life."[4] That's a whole lot more than a covering, right? It is the divine influence of God's nature that embodies us, issued from Holy Spirit like a heartbeat gives a fresh pump of oxygenated blood every second or so. This divine nature manifests in many ways in our daily life when we stand firm in our new identity and fix our mind on the truth of who we are. When we understand our new righteous nature and ignore any lie that would rob us of this truth, grace powerfully causes it to become our experiential reality.

This is why Paul told Timothy to be strong in the grace of God (2 Timothy 2:1). Grace is something we become strong in, by understanding what Jesus accomplished on our behalf. It cannot empower our self-effort but manifests in the humble (James 4:6). It cannot manifest in the proud who would seek a righteousness to manifest through their efforts. Grace will not empower dead works, or it would reinforce our efforts as though they were valid for righteousness.

Grace is not designed to enable anything apart from simple, intentional faith.

KNOWING THE GRACE OF GOD IN TRUTH

Is grace truly the entire foundational means of fruitfulness in our Christian lives once we understand our new nature? We know Paul claimed grace was the key ingredient to his actions as he walked in Holy Spirit. But what about the rest of us? Look here at what Paul also describes as the source of the fruitfulness in the entire church at Colossae:

> *"Since we heard of your faith in Christ Jesus and of the love that you have for all the saints, because of the hope laid up for you in heaven. Of this you have heard before in the word of the truth, the gospel, which has come to you, as indeed in the whole world it is bearing fruit and increasing—as it also does among you, since the day you heard it and understood the grace of God in truth."*
> **COLOSSIANS 1:4-6**

We must embrace the message of the gospel, Christ and His crucifixion, and our joint death and resurrection with Him. But it can have powerfully tangible effects once we also "understand the grace of God in truth." Here we learn that when we understand grace in truth, the gospel bears fruit in our lives by that grace. Grace is not a covering for you to be hidden from God and stay in your sin, it is the power to honor him with your new life in Christ. Grace reigns through righteousness because that is your new nature (Romans 5:17, 21).

> *Grace cannot empower you to sin because your nature is not to sin anymore. It can only empower who you really are.*

When I fixed my heart and mind on the truth that I was a son now—free from the old, sinful nature—it was not long before I got into a situation that in the past would have caused me to manifest anger or self-defense.

Because I had fixed my attention and understanding on what God says I am now in Christ and constantly enjoyed the intimacy with the Father these things provide, all that manifested was the fruit of the Spirit! I did not have to stir it up or pretend to be nice because I was a Christian. Grace empowered my understanding in Christ to manifest, and I walked victoriously through the circumstance. This is how the new covenant Christian life is supposed to function.

YOUR HOT NEW CAR

Picture your new righteous nature as a car. Holy Spirit is the builder and provider of that beautiful car in the regeneration workshop. All you do is show up and collect it (get born again) from the grace garage, trading in your old, beat-up, "sinful nature" car. Best trade ever! Holy Spirit then pumps the premium grace fuel that sits in the tank of your new car and makes the whole thing move. This fuel will never run out! It is your understanding and faith in the truth that stomps that pedal down so that grace can finally do its thing and you can reign in this life.

Paul compelled us to not receive the grace of God in vain (2 Corinthians 6:1; Galatians 2:21). How do you do that? If the grace of God has come abundantly to you (John 1:16; Romans 5:2), but then you try to make yourself righteous by other means, or you choose not to engage in an intentionally holy lifestyle, then even though you have grace living inside you, it will lie dormant. You will have received grace in vain. Grace can only empower your new nature by your faith and understanding. Do not try to be righteous in your efforts. That is like trying to design, build, and provide your car and then push it down the road by your strength. How tiring!

Do not strive for a nature the Lord has already given you.

Thank God for who you are now and that *you* can be expressed as you lean on the truth and set your mind on these things. Put into action the things you learn about who you are in Scripture by stepping out and behaving as if you are what He says you are. You will find it is the most natural thing to do because it *is* who you are. You have an endless capacity to look just like Jesus, to exhibit the fruit of the Spirit, to embrace His ways, and to know the Father with great enjoyment!

Righteousness will become a burden to you if you do not understand it is enabled by grace and oiled by intimacy. The people I know who live the holiest lives are the ones who are also the most restful and peaceful. They are those who have put all their chips on grace and righteousness, and they are rooted in a relationship with God. I have also found it is more tiring and frustrating to live in sin than it is to live in holiness. Fight the good fight of *faith*, not a fight of works. You must not let the enemy trick you into condemnation. This will cause you to put off grace and try to achieve your holiness. This will not free you from sin; it ultimately causes sin.

Let grace reign through righteousness in your life. Grace is an enabling reality, empowering you to live a holy life and to be yourself in Christ, which means you can never use the term as a reason for staying in sin. You are not under law but under grace, to live free from sin's dominion (Romans 6:14). I pray the awakening to righteousness will be increasingly known for its grace-enabled holiness, marked by a supernatural peace and ease.

Righteousness is enabled by grace and oiled by intimacy

(ENDNOTES)

1. St. Augustine of Hippo, Philip Schaff, ed., *Saint Augustine's Anti-Pelagian Writings* (Annotated Edition) (Jazzybee Verlag, 2012).
2. William D. Mounce, "Grace," *Mounce's Complete Expository Dictionary of Old and New Testament Words* (Zondervan; Supersaver ed. Edition, 2006).
3. *Strong's* G4052
4. *Strong's* G5485

CHAPTER 13
RIGHTLY DIVIDING THE WORD

Many Christians have a love/hate relationship with the Scriptures. We know we are called to be mighty in them (Acts 18:24) and to let them dwell in us richly (Colossians 3:16), but too often we read them with the wrong lens. When we should find encouragement, instruction in righteousness, absolute truth to hold to in our circumstances, liberty from sin, and insight into our identity, we often end up condemned and confused by our times in the Bible instead.

We have moved from darkness to light, from sinners to righteous saints. We must examine the lens we look at Scripture through now that we have discovered our new identity. As we have seen, one main theme of the Bible is righteousness: righteousness for the sake of intimacy with God and the expression of His will on the earth, purchased and delivered by Jesus Christ and empowered in our lives by the grace of God. It has been hidden in plain sight, yet many of us have missed it. Here, again, are strong and overarching statements about righteousness being the key message of the Scriptures:

- *All* the Scriptures train and teach us about righteousness (2 Timothy 3:16).

- Scriptures tell us to seek God's righteousness first (Matthew 6:33).

- Paul says the reason the gospel is so powerful is because the righteousness of God is revealed in it (Romans 1:16–17).

- Scripture calls itself the "word of righteousness" (Hebrews 5:13), commanding us to become skilled in it.

- One fundamental reason Jesus became a man was to make it possible for us to become the righteousness of God (2 Corinthians 5:21).

- The reason He died on the cross was so we would die to sin and live to righteousness (1 Peter 2:24).

- Jesus was the end of the law-based righteousness that could not save us in the old covenant, giving us His righteousness in the new covenant (Romans 10:4).

The Scriptures are a divine commentary on the covenant journey that man and God embarked on together after man's fall in the garden. This journey came finally to a place where God's righteousness could be given to us in the only way it would ever really work: apart from our effort and input, received by faith alone. The Scriptures tell the story of man's personal and failed pursuit of righteousness and God's ultimate provision of righteousness, *all for the sake of intimacy and relationship.*

The Scriptures are under spiritual attack in our modern culture. In fact, they have been attacked consistently throughout history. Too many Christians have believed a lie that the Scriptures are irrelevant, too difficult to understand, or not inspired by God. We had no access to the Scriptures for many centuries as common Christians, while many gave their lives to put it into the hands of the masses. Today however, we face an opposite problem. Our bookshelves (and mobile devices) are filled with a whole range of Bibles, but *many have lost their belief in the integrity, authority, and inspiration of Scripture.* This is a demonic attack against the church, undermining the power of the Word. We must stand against it.

"Sanctify them in the truth; your word is truth."
JOHN 17:17

We need a revival of value for the Scriptures in our generation. It is the divinely inspired message of God to humanity. It contains the absolute truth. Sure, it must be read in its right context, and this can take a little time to get comfortable with, but it can and must be done.

False prophets are a hot topic of conversation in the church today, but the Bible equally warns us about false teachers (2 Peter 2:1–3; 2 Timothy 4:1–22; 1 Timothy 4:1; Romans 16:17). We must take responsibility as individuals for our understanding of Scripture. Doctrine matters. It determines how we understand God, how we live our lives, treat our spouses, raise our kids, share the gospel, make disciples, and understand the world. It determines everything, and it comes from *Scripture.* We can never blame our leaders if they did not teach us correct things from the Bible when we *all* have access to the Word of God and are filled with Holy Spirit, who longs to teach and lead us into *all truth* (John 16:13).

The awakening to righteousness must bring with it a new love for the integrity and inspiration of Scripture. This is a pursuit of understanding and is led by Scripture alone in our lives, filtering everything we hear from the pulpit through the Word. We must teach the rising generation how to be mighty in the Scriptures. When we rightly define ourselves by Christ alone, we can finally have discussions about theology that don't end with disunity and new denominations.

Here is truth to expose a common lie. *The Bible is not hard to understand.* There are a few keys that make it easy to read in intimacy with God and give it direct application to our lives. Here is the first key to keep in mind:

The Word is a mirror, not a measure.

When taking hold of the reality of righteousness, you learn that for Christians, the Word is a *mirror,* not a measure. You see your renewed self in the reflection of Jesus's life. You can then learn to function in this truth by grace. The Bible is not something you measure yourself by; it is something you discover yourself in and hold fast to.

Does the Bible teach this? Of course:

> *"But be doers of the word, and not hearers only, deceiving yourselves. For if anyone is a hearer of the word and not a doer, he is like a man who looks intently at his natural face in a mirror. For he looks at himself and goes away and at once forgets what he was like."*
>
> **JAMES 1:22-24**

When you look into the Word, it is the same as looking at your natural face in a mirror. Studying the Scriptures gives us a better look at who we now are in Christ.

Also:

> *"But we all, with unveiled face, beholding as in a mirror the glory of the Lord, are being transformed into the same image from glory to glory, just as by the Spirit of the Lord."*
>
> **2 CORINTHIANS 3:18**

So how should we read the Old Testament? How should we read the Gospels? How should we read the Epistles? The lens through which we read and interpret Scripture is critical to understanding the gospel correctly and walking in freedom as saints. Let's look now at each major section of the Scriptures and see a couple of keys for rightly dividing them in context, covenant, and application. This will help you pursue living a life mighty in the Scriptures, and you can teach others to do the same.

THE OLD TESTAMENT

> *"Do your best to present yourself to God as one approved, a worker who has no need to be ashamed, rightly handling the word of truth."*
>
> **2 TIMOTHY 2:15**

If we are not diligent to rightly handle the context, covenant, and application of Scripture, we might limit the finished work of Jesus by misinterpreting the Old Testament. For example, in the book of Esther, Esther had to spend six months bathing and preparing to spend a night with the king. Does this mean we have to teach new Christians to embrace a symbolic spiritual cleansing for six months before being with Jesus? Of course not. We also saw already how wrongly applying King David's cry for a new heart to ourselves can limit us from embracing our new hearts in the new covenant. We must learn to rightly divide the word of truth so that we do not rob Jesus of what He paid for and miss out on our intimacy and freedom.

Remember this; the Old must be read *through* the New.

Here are some keys to have in mind as you approach Old Testament Scripture:

- The Old Testament points to righteousness. The New Testament provides righteousness.

- The Old Testament intends to make you wise for salvation through faith in Jesus Christ (2 Timothy 3:15).

- It also is useful for teaching, reproof, correction, and training in righteousness (2 Timothy 3:16).

- The entire Bible, including the Old Testament, concerns *Jesus*. He is the object of Scripture (Romans 1:2; Luke. 24:27).

- We can read the Old Testament accounts as encouraging *examples* of faith (Hebrews 11; Romans 4).

In the Old Testament, we learn the depth of man's need for salvation and man's helplessness—without a pure heart and clear conscience before God. We see Adam's fall in the garden, which was the beginning of man's brokenness. We then see God set humanity on a path of redemption, leading us slowly back to His heart through covenant relationships, revealing types and shadows, throughout, of the redemption we would receive finally in Christ. His ultimate desire is to be our God, while we are His people alone. His desire is to be known intimately by every individual.

Once Jesus came on the scene in the New Testament, we could see Him everywhere in the Old Testament too. Jesus showed up and gave us our proper reading glasses for understanding everything that happened in the Old Testament. We could not accurately know God's ways in the Old Testament until Jesus had come and given us insight into His nature and intentions. In fact, when Jesus arrived on the scene, He boldly stated: "No one knows the Father except the Son" (Matthew 11:27). All our best religious efforts were futile in understanding God or becoming righteous before Him, because of the veil of our sinful nature. God became flesh to reveal Himself fully to us and to fix the sin problem. The Old Testament helps us learn that sharing God's righteousness in Christ is the only way to be free and have union with God, and that Christ is the full revelation of the God who created us.

If you are wondering whether the Old Testament is as relevant or inspired as the New, then you must look ultimately at how much value Jesus and the apostles put on the Old Testament. Jesus quoted the Old Testament at least seventy-eight times and the Pentateuch alone twenty-six times. He referred to the Old Testament as "the Scriptures" (John 10:35), "the word of God" (Mark 7:13), and the "commandment of God" (Matthew 15:3). He also said the Scriptures could not be broken or altered (John 10:35), referring to the Old Testament (although this includes the New Testament as well). The apostles quoted about two hundred and nine times from the Old Testament and considered it "the oracles of God" (Hebrews 5:12; Romans 3:2) and the Scriptures. In hundreds of places, the Old Testament predicted the events of the New Testament. Because the New Testament is the fulfillment of, and testifies to, the authenticity of the Old Testament, both Testaments must be considered together equally as the Word of God.

We must value the entire Bible in the same way. The red letters are no more or less inspired than the book of Leviticus or Romans. Holy Spirit equally spoke and declared the message of God through every page.

It is not a question of inspiration when we look at the various portions of Scripture. It is a question of context and covenant.

For example, if you want to know how God feels about man, Jesus is the best representation, not the book of Jonah. When Jonah is read through a lens of Jesus's revelation of the Father, you see an incredible message of God's patience and desire for man to know Him start to shine through the story. Likewise, we must look at the new covenant, not the old covenant, to know what God's eternal desire is. Scripture teaches us this.

Even Jesus revealed that all the Old Testament words were ultimately pointing to Him.

Look at this profound passage, showing what Jesus said on the road to Emmaus to two disciples whom His appearance was hidden from, shortly after His resurrection. They were confused about why the one they thought was their Messiah ended up nailed to the cross instead of liberating them, through violence, from Roman oppression. Jesus referred to the Old Testament and said:

> *"O foolish ones, and slow of heart to believe all that the*
> *prophets have spoken! Was it not necessary that the Christ*
> *should suffer these things and enter into his glory?" And*
> *beginning with Moses and all the Prophets, he interpreted to*
> *them in all the Scriptures the things concerning himself."*
> **LUKE 24:25-27**

Wow! Jesus took *all* the Old Testament Scriptures and showed these two (extremely lucky) disciples that in every Scripture, He was the ultimate topic. Jesus is the Word made flesh (John 1:14), the beginning and the end (Revelation 22:13). He is the reason for life. The Bible is *all* about Him.

As we saw in chapter 11, if what you get out of the Old Testament is not validated in, or consistent with, the New Testament regarding God's nature, righteousness, faith, and salvation, then what you got out of the Old Testament probably needs clarifying. If you misapply Scripture, it can severely limit your life in God and your freedom in His love through Christ.

Here are key verses from the New Testament which give us a healthy lens to look through when reading the Old Testament:

> *"And how from childhood you have been acquainted with the*
> *sacred writings, which are able to make you wise for salvation*

through faith in Christ Jesus. All Scripture is breathed out by God and profitable for teaching, for reproof, for correction, and for training in righteousness, that the man of God may be complete, equipped for every good work."
2 TIMOTHY 3:15-17

This says *all* Scripture is breathed out by God, not some! This same "all Scripture" goes even further though. It is useful for teaching us about *righteousness*! It points to salvation in Christ, makes us complete, and equips us for every good work. These are good things to be looking for as you read the Old Testament.

"But now the righteousness of God has been manifested apart from the law, although the Law and the Prophets bear witness to it."
ROMANS 3:21

The Law and the Prophets of the Old Testament bear witness to righteousness. They point to the promise.

"Paul, a servant of Christ Jesus, called to be an apostle, set apart for the gospel of God, which he promised beforehand through his prophets in the holy Scriptures, concerning his Son, who was descended from David according to the flesh and was declared to be the Son of God in power according to the Spirit of holiness by his resurrection from the dead, Jesus Christ our Lord,"
ROMANS 1:1-4

The Scriptures concern the Son of God! The Old Testament is the inspired Word of God.

- It shows us God's creative nature and narrative.
- It documents the beginning of our existence.
- It shows us the origin of man's problem and gives the promise of an answer. It points to Jesus. It points to righteousness.

- It shows us God's goodness as He leads us throughout history into the new covenant and eternal life.

- It teaches us to be faithful and to trust His goodness.

- It gives us incredible examples of God's response to man's faithfulness and God's faithfulness to man.

Read it right, and you will learn to love it. Look for Jesus on every page, as for hidden treasure!

THE GOSPELS

Do you know the new covenant does not start at the birth of Jesus? Jesus modeled the new covenant life for three years, but only once He turned thirty. He then made it accessible for all at His death and resurrection. It was inaugurated for man by the outpouring of the Spirit on the day of Pentecost (Acts 2). There is a very specific context Jesus lived in. He was born "under the law" (Galatians 4:4). He lived in the context of the old covenant and dealt with people who were still bound to that covenant while pointing them (and us) to the new covenant He was exemplifying.

The Gospels are the account of the incarnated God, speaking directly to us and modeling the life we can embrace as Christians. It helps us to understand the context Jesus lived and functioned in when reading His life and words. There are also occasions in the Gospels when we need the Epistles to give us clarity and further understanding, which we will examine.

*"But when the fullness of time had come, God sent forth his
Son, born of woman, born under the law."*

GALATIANS 4:4

THE SERMON ON THE MOUNT

To show an example of this, let's look at the Sermon on the Mount (Matthew 5–7). Jesus had a twofold way of dealing with people. What He taught in this sermon applies to both the old and new covenants. To those who read it looking back from the new covenant, with insight into Jesus's redemptive work on the cross, He prophesied what a new heart, empowered by grace and filled with Holy Spirit, was capable of. This new heart is capable of pure motives as we engage in Christian disciplines, walk in love, honor God and people, have purity in our hearts regarding lust and anger, etc. But for those listening in the context of the old covenant, He was making it impossible for them to think they could be righteous under the law.

While revealing what the redeemed Christian expression of being empowered by grace would look like, Jesus brought the existing mindset toward the law under serious fault. Good intentions did not save the Pharisees, and a special right was not given to the Jews because God chose them. He made it officially impossible to behold righteousness apart from grace and the new covenant. For those who thought they were doing okay under the law—not committing adultery or hating their brothers, Jesus claimed adultery and hatred even applied to the desires of the heart, not just the act.

This sermon once for all destroyed the idea of striving for righteousness under the law. Jesus finally went as far as saying "You therefore must be perfect, as your heavenly Father is perfect" (Matthew 5:48). Imagine hearing this as those under the law, though, being ignorant of the death and resurrection coming to give them access to God's perfection. How discouraging! Even if they could have achieved the demands of the law, they could never be perfect like God! This sermon would have crippled anyone hearing it through the ear of the law. For us looking back through the lens of the Epistles and the clarity of the apostles' insight into the new covenant, we know He has perfected us by His grace (Hebrews 10:14). When we look back through the redemption of the cross and what it has done in our nature, we can be excited to see how it is possible to live in the likeness of Jesus's life in the Gospels—completely by grace.

THE TRUE GREAT COMMANDMENT:

Here is a great example of rightly dividing the Word. We have taught for some time in the church we are to fulfill the two greatest commandments of the Judaic law: "Love the Lord your God with all your heart and soul and mind and strength, and love your neighbor as yourself" (Matthew 22:34–40). But let's look at the context of these laws when Jesus quoted them (also Mark 12:30 and Luke 10:27):

> *"But when the Pharisees heard that he had silenced the Sadducees, they gathered together. And one of them, a lawyer, asked him a question to test him. "Teacher, which is the great commandment in the Law?" And he said to him, "You shall love the Lord your God with all your heart and with all your soul and with all your mind. This is the great and first commandment. And a second is like it: You shall love your neighbor as yourself. On these two commandments depend all the Law and the Prophets."*
>
> **MATTHEW 22:34-40**

Here, Jesus was asked a question about the Jewish law, so Jesus answered accordingly, even though it was about a law that no longer applies to Christians. We live under the law of love and liberty now (James 2:8, 12). We are no longer under old covenant law, but under grace (Romans 6:14). Christ was the last stop of the law for righteousness—for us who believe (Romans 10:4). The Judaic law is obsolete to us. It is only laid down for the unrighteous, not those who have become righteous under the new covenant (1 Timothy 1:9).

So what is the commandment we live by in the new covenant?

> *"A new commandment I give to you, that you love one another:*
> *just as I have loved you, you also are to love one another."*
> **JOHN 13:34**

> *"This is my commandment, that you love one another as*
> *I have loved you."*
> **JOHN 15:12**

As you can see, a new covenant gets a new command. The love referred to in the Jewish law quoted above is a love we must produce by our strength for God and others. Look at who the full emphasis is on to perform: *You* must love the Lord your God with all *your* heart and *your* soul and *your* mind and *your* strength. Jesus had said no one knew the Father (Matthew 11:27), so how on earth could they love Him this way if they did not even know Him? That is the whole point. The law reveals our complete inability to be whole, holy, or acceptable to God. This new law of love, however, starts with His love for us! "As *I have loved you,* you also are to love one another." This finally gives us a model of real love because Jesus has shown it to us! Our job is to receive it and develop an understanding of it. When we embrace this love, it will pour forth onto the creation around us as a response to our union with the person who is love!

Also, see these verses on the topic:

> *"And this is his commandment, that we believe in the name*
> *of his Son Jesus Christ and love one another, just as he has*
> *commanded us."*
> **1 JOHN 3:23**

> *"Then they said to him, 'What must we do, to be doing the*
> *works of God?' Jesus answered them, 'This is the work of God,*

that you believe in him whom he has sent.'"
JOHN 6:28-29

What Jesus was teaching in His summary of the law's greatest commandments (Matthew 22:34-40) is that it is impossible to love the Lord your God with all your heart, soul, mind, and strength unless you discover and believe His love for you first. He was compelling those under the law to come to the end of themselves, to finally humble themselves and recognize their desperate need for a savior. Only then could the love the Son showed them become the same love we can embody and display to the world.

"For the law was given through Moses; grace and truth came through Jesus Christ."
JOHN 1:17

The Gospels, just like all Scripture, must be read through a proper lens of historical context. A good consideration is this: if a Scripture you read means something different to you than to the original reader or writer, then you may be off topic. Always look for the original meaning, then you can better apply it to your life. Let's now look at how the Epistles can be an incredible help in our understanding of the rest of Scripture.

THE EPISTLES

"We need the same Spirit to understand the Scripture, which enabled the holy men of old to write it."
JOHN WESLEY[1]

Remember, there is no hierarchy of quality in Scripture. The entire book is equally inspired. We are examining context and covenant chronology here so we can get the right things from Scripture when we read.

Jesus told the disciples that he had not spoken everything they needed to hear about the truth, in His lifetime on earth, but that the Spirit of truth would come and teach them all truth (John 14:26). This means the incarnated God told us, and it's recorded in the Gospels, there was more we needed to learn. He told us we would need more insight into His life and words and more understanding of the new covenant, but it was Holy Spirit who would teach us this.

When did the Spirit of truth come? He came when the Epistles were written. The Epistles were written with Holy Spirit by people who were now born again, having unhindered insight into the new covenant Jesus had pointed to.

Holy Spirit is the one who inspired the writers of the Epistles, just as He did the writers of the Gospels and the Old Testament. Paul stated strongly the mystery of God was revealed fully to him, and he wrote this mystery powerfully in his letters, as did the authors of the other Epistles. We could not understand Jesus's command to be perfect, for example (Matthew 5:48), if we did not have Hebrews 10:14 and Romans 6 teaching us that our baptism into His death and resurrection perfected us!

> *We must look at the Old Testament and the Gospels with the insight of the Epistles to have an accurate and whole understanding of all the Scriptures.*

The verses below show that we can find the reality of the new covenant explained in the Epistles:

> *"These things I have spoken to you while I am still with you. But the Helper, the Holy Spirit, whom the Father will send in my name, He will teach you all things and bring to your remembrance all that I have said to you."*
>
> **JOHN 14:25-26**

> *"I still have many things to say to you, but you cannot bear them now. When the Spirit of truth comes, He will guide you into all the truth, for He will not speak on his own authority, but whatever He hears He will speak, and He will declare to you the things that are to come."*
>
> **JOHN 16:12-13**

See here how Jesus declared He could not tell the disciples all they needed to hear but Holy Spirit would, once they could understand—after the cross.

> *"Of which I became a minister according to the stewardship from God that was given to me for you, to make the word of God fully known, the mystery hidden for ages and generations but now revealed to his saints."*
>
> **COLOSSIANS 1:25-26**

> *"When you read this, you can perceive my insight into the mystery of Christ, which was not made known to the sons of men in other generations as it has now been revealed to his holy apostles and prophets by the Spirit."*
>
> **EPHESIANS 3:4-5**

> *"I have said these things to you in figures of speech. The hour is coming when I will no longer speak to you in figures of speech but will tell you plainly about the Father."*
>
> **JOHN 16:25**

> *"In hope of eternal life, which God, who never lies, promised before the ages began and at the proper time manifested in his word through the preaching with which I have been entrusted by the command of God our Savior"*
>
> **TITUS 1:2-3**

These verses give us insight into the immense new covenant clarity of the Epistles. They are an essential guide for understanding the rest of Scripture.

God can also speak to us from Scripture, apart from its original context. But this will never be inconsistent with the explicit context and message of the whole counsel of Scripture. His Word is always the final authority. We must use the keys we have just looked at to grow in the Scriptures with Holy Spirit. I encourage you to do this prayerfully and diligently, always in a place of intimacy with the Father and with thankfulness for the glorious truth you find.

Enjoy the discovery of your new identity in Christ and the intimacy you have access to through His perfect sacrifice on the cross. The Scriptures will become a cherished thing to you, a daily experience with the truth of the gospel, with increasing evidence in your life of the glorious truth you discover!

(ENDNOTES)

1. John Wesley, John Emory, *The Works of the Rev. John Wesley,* Volume 5 (New York: Carlton & Phillips, 1853), 468.

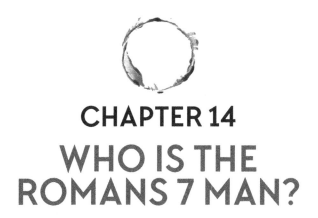

CHAPTER 14
WHO IS THE ROMANS 7 MAN?

THE WRETCHED MAN

The radical truth of our new righteous life in Christ is being preached in diverse circles. Often, the same few Scripture passages come up when question time comes around. These are very important questions for which there are accurate answers. "What about Romans 7?" "What about Paul claiming he was chief of sinners?" "Didn't Paul say, 'I die daily'? Does that mean we are dying to the old man slowly?" "Doesn't 1 John 1 say we are deceived if we say we have no sin?"

We must properly interpret these few Scripture passages that have been a hindrance for many as they hear the truth of their new nature in Christ. The "I die daily" comment can be solved by reading the entire chapter you find it in (1 Corinthians 15) and understanding the context. Ironically, it is all about righteousness, not an argument against it. The "chief of sinners" comment is similar, as we already saw in part 1.

As for 1 John 1:8–9, I encourage you to take the previous chapter on rightly dividing the word of truth and study 1 John for yourself. Read the Epistle with the lens of righteousness I have spoken of and you will find clear, contextual answers to your questions. Studying the Scriptures is a very important practice to prioritize in an age when we can get answers so readily. We must each make the truth our own, learning to delve into the Scriptures and become convinced of the gospel in our hearts.

The passage I consider to be the most devastating to misunderstand is Romans 7:14–25. It has held countless Christians in an identity crisis. Let's examine the "wretched Romans 7 man." Without a proper context in mind as we read, Romans 7 can seem to be describing the normal Christian experience: a battle with sin that can never truly end in this life, because sin remains part of our post-conversion nature (v. 17, v. 20). The problem is this drastically contradicts the explicit message of Paul's Epistle: that we are no longer under sin's dominion. We were set free from the sin nature when we were co-crucified with Christ (Romans 6:6; Colossians 3:3; Galatians 2:20; 2 Corinthians 5:21).

Another problem is that the Romans 7 man is not experiencing an occasional experience of sin, but an utter defeat by sin (v. 14, v. 24). If we conclude that Romans 7 is the Christian experience, then we must agree we are "carnal," "sold under sin," and "wretched" to the core. We are destined for failure, slaves to a life of sinfulness not very distinguishable to that of unbelievers. If it's true, then we must make the conclusion that we are left in the same state as before we were born again, remaining subject to the Jewish law (another huge confusion for modern gentiles), and we cannot expect liberation from sin in this life. This is what Romans 7:14–25 means if we believe it refers to the Christian experience.

Not exactly good news, right? The true message of the new covenant, as we have seen, is that we are now light with no darkness (Ephesians 5:8). We are new creations, with the old nature gone and the new fully come (2 Corinthians 5:17). We are partakers of the divine nature (2 Peter 1:3), free from sin (Romans 6:2–7; 11–18, 22), and saints (over sixty verses). These powerful statements of our identity must be explained away as positional or theoretical if we embrace that Romans 7 represents the Christian experience.

Many early Church Fathers thought these verses described an unregenerate, non-Christian person. This was Augustine's early view too, but partly because of his battle with Pelagius over some heretical teaching, he changed his opinion and decided the person depicted in these verses was a Christian.[1] This interpretation was adopted by many of the Reformers, influenced greatly by Augustine's ideas. Luther put more weight on this than the rest, who saw in these verses the classic statement of his view of the believer as "at the same time a justified person and a sinner" (*simul iustus et peccator*). Luther concluded that justification, being an entirely forensic declaration of the believer's status before God, did not remove the presence and influence of sin from the believer. (See chapter sixteen for more on this.)

The key reason some modern scholars still conclude Paul was speaking about the Christian experience in Romans 7 is because of a stance that the sinful nature still indwells believers. When the "sinner saved by grace" lens is removed, it is evident this is not the correct conclusion. If you could ask a dozen New Testament scholars to list the five most difficult passages in the New Testament, I am sure most would include Romans 7:14–25 on their list. There have been strongly opposing views over the years on this passage.[2]

MY ROMANS 7 CHAPTER

I had a striking resemblance to this Romans 7 man before I discovered the truth. But we must never let our experience determine truth for us.

> *Scripture must dictate truth to us, and then our experience will submit itself to the truth as we learn to embrace it by faith, despite what our experience might try to declare on the matter.*

I was traveling in India, four years into my Christian faith, struggling deeply with sin, lust, drinking too much, selfishness, pride, and much more. I was a new creation from the day of my conversion but was living a deceived life. Without the knowledge of righteousness and the finished work of Jesus on my behalf, I was living nearly as lost as I had lived before I met Jesus. Only now I had a new heart and the divine nature living inside me, yearning to live in its holy state, so I was far more miserable when I sinned, being no longer compatible with it. I believed I was a "sinner saved by grace," and so my experience was one of sin and turmoil. One day, while traveling on the famous Indian train lines, I was reading my Bible and came across Romans 7 for the first time.

I read Paul's present tense, first-person words about doing what he did not want to do and not doing what he wanted to do (v. 15, v. 19). I read his comments about being a wretched man, sold under sin (v. 14, v. 24). I found myself strangely comforted as I read, concluding Paul must have had the same experience I was having. *Paul also lived a life of struggle with sin,* I thought. *He was also defeated by it constantly, even though he did not want to be.* I had not found an answer that could free me from sin, but I thought I had a mutual experience with Paul, and that was comforting in a way.

I slumped back into the "Romans 7 sofa," a place of comfort in sin, a place of resolving that sin was just a lifelong battle to resign myself to. If the amazing apostle Paul struggled with sin to the degree he mentioned in Romans 7, then I was obviously destined to as well. I resolved that God was a forgiving God, and by His grace and mercy, He would always love me *in* my sin, but He had not saved me *from* my sin. I resigned myself to knowing there was no way to be free from sin in this life. At best, I could slightly progress in sanctification and make small ground in holiness. For the rest of my life, I would just need to continually ask forgiveness and be happy with a future promise of liberation. I was comforted because I had an answer for my experience finally—a disempowering one, but an answer.

SAVED FROM THE SOFA

When a message of an imparted nature of righteousness found its way to me some time later, I had to have my fingers pried off my Romans 7 comfort. I was thrown off the sofa. Because of my long history with sin and having defined myself as a sinner still, my life had continued to digress. I had come to a place of complacency in sin, even though I did not have an enjoyable experience in life and was powerless to overcome sin. The problem with sin is it is never satisfied, it takes and takes from us with an insatiable appetite, hence the continual digression.

I then had a powerful experience with God one day, while being prayed for. I was set free of things I thought I would never be free from in this life. I heard a message of identity in Christ and my adoption as a son. I saw righteousness on every page of my Bible, and not merely as a future promise, but as a present tense inheritance. I had to humble myself and reconsider my conclusions of Romans 7.

I had to acknowledge that perhaps my experience had interpreted Scripture for me, instead of Scripture dictating and transforming my experience.

I know many who read this will have a similar association with Romans 7, and if still in that place, are having a battle with sin right now. I can boldly say: the battle was won on the cross! Remember how the Lamb of God saved us from our sin, not in our sin (John 1:29)? Having discovered the reality of the finished work and the proper context of Romans 7, I could finally embrace the explicit message of righteousness and walk free from sin.

I do not deny that Christians can struggle with sin, but I strongly deny that this Romans 7 passage describes that struggle. Romans 7, as we will see, describes the battle of a person under the law, one who is not yet born again. Christians can deal with far less of a struggle than we have believed. I still feel the temptation to sin and have stumbled too, but now I see sin for what it is: It's outside me, trying to make me submit to its deception. It wants to reign in my mortal body, but I do not have to let it (Romans 6:12).

God removed sin from our nature but not from the earth. Sin has a way of trying to convince us we have not changed and aims to rule in our lives by deceiving us. If we expect a constant battle with sin as Christians, guess what? Sin will take opportunity through our misunderstanding. Our experience will continue to reinforce our idea that Romans 7 is the Christian life, because that is where our faith has rested.

I can boldly say I live a life of liberty that would offend and confuse many who live under a sinner paradigm. It is not because I am trying harder—if anything, I am trying less. It is because of this revelation. I know many others who enjoy this freedom too.

When you discover His righteousness, freely imparted as a redeemed nature, you gain access to a life of intimacy with the Father that will overwhelm you. Once you recognize that He recreated *you* in His perfect likeness, any opposing feeling or thought can be distinguished from your new nature. You will truly rest in Father God and deeply enjoy your union with Him.

INEXCUSABLE INCONSISTENCIES

Here are three huge inconsistencies we must explain if we maintain the Romans 7 experience is the Christian experience:

Inconsistency #1

> *"For while we were (past tense) living in the flesh, our sinful passions, aroused by the law, were (past tense) at work in our members to bear fruit for death."*
> **ROMANS 7:5**

Inconsistent with:

> *"But I see in my members another law waging war against the law of my mind and making me captive to the law of sin that dwells in my members."*
> **ROMANS 7:23**

In verse 5, we see sinful passions *were* (past tense) at work in our members when we *were* (past tense) in the flesh. This distinguishes our past bondage from our current freedom. In verse 23, we see Paul stated the opposite of verse 5, that the law of sin was still very much in his members.

If Paul spoke of his current experience in verse 14–25, where first person language was used, then he contradicted himself with opposite themes here. When referring to Christians, the "flesh" is not something that can scripturally be defined as the sinful nature, or as an evil facet of the Christian. It is an oft-misunderstood term. There has been great controversy over one key Bible translation that has interpreted the word in such a way, attracting great criticism and sadly confusing many. The "flesh," translated for the Greek word *sarx*, referring to the "old man" in Scripture, was circumcised once for all by the crucifixion of Christ (Colossians 2:11). If the Spirit of God dwells in you, then the flesh does not (Romans 8:9). Galatians 5:24

tells us "anyone who is in Christ *has* crucified the flesh, with its desires." Where the word is used synonymously with the sinful nature, it has clearly been crucified with Christ. The same Greek word is also used in other ways though. We now have a neutral flesh, referring to our physical human body, using the same Greek word (Ephesians 5:29). We also have an ability to think according to the flesh (Romans 8:6, also see *sarkikos*, 1 Corinthians 3:3); this refers to carnal thinking. However, we no longer have the flesh where the term refers to the old nature.[3] As you can see, there is a stark contradiction in these two verses in Romans 7.

Inconsistency #2

"For he who has died has been freed from sin."

ROMANS 6:7

"And having been set free from sin, you became slaves of righteousness."

ROMANS 6:18

"But now having been set free from sin, and having become slaves of God, you have your fruit to holiness, and the end, everlasting life."

ROMANS 6:22

"For one who has died has been set free from sin."

ROMANS 6:7

"So you also must consider yourselves dead to sin and alive to God in Christ Jesus."

ROMANS 6:11

"For sin will have no dominion over you, since you are not under law but under grace."

ROMANS 6:14

"But thanks be to God, that you who were (Past tense) once slaves of sin have become obedient from the heart to the standard of teaching to which you were committed."

ROMANS 6:17

"For when you were (past tense) slaves of sin, you were free in regard to righteousness."

ROMANS 6:20

Inconsistent with:

"For we know that the law is spiritual, but I am of the flesh, sold under sin."

ROMANS 7:14

The whole chapter of Romans 6 declares our freedom from sin to the point of repetitiveness. In Romans 7:14, however, the man describes himself as sold under sin. Are we free from sin or still sold under it? We cannot be both. Paul cannot be referring to the Christian experience in Romans 7.

Inconsistency #3

"But I see in my members another law waging war against the law of my mind and making me captive to the law of sin that dwells in my members."

ROMANS 7:23

Inconsistent with:

"For the law of the Spirit of life has set you free in Christ Jesus from the law of sin and death."

ROMANS 8:2

Remember, there were no chapter breaks in Paul's original letter. Here in Romans 7:23, Paul said he was in captivity to the law of sin. However, Paul's conclusion of the Romans 7 message, four verses later in Romans 8:2, says we are free from the law of sin by the Spirit of life in Christ. A huge inconsistency.

On top of these inexcusable inconsistencies is that the Romans 7 man, in these verses, struggles with the need to obey the Mosaic law; yet Paul had already taught the release of the believer from the law (6:14; 7:4–6). This is a huge confusion for many Christians, creating far-reaching issues of legalism. Many misunderstand the clear division between the old and new covenants because of wrongly interpreting Romans 7.

Multiple modern commentators agree Paul was not referring to the Christian experience in Romans 7:14–25. It has been more common historically for theologians to interpret the passage this way.[4] Dodd, Moffatt, and Wesley are three good examples of this. Luther and Calvin ultimately decided it was the Christian experience, but admitted a struggle to reconcile the strong slavery to sin pictured in the passage.[5] This has led to widespread support in the West for this view. It creates far too many unexplainable inconsistencies, though, as we have seen, not to mention the blatant opposition it creates to the explicit message of Scripture: that in Christ we have moved from death to life. Douglas J. Moo is an exceptional and reputable commentator on the Epistle to the Romans, for those wanting to get more insight and clarity on this view.[6]

IF YOU ARE NOT THE ROMANS 7 MAN, WHO IS?

Let's look at an overview of Romans 5–8 to get a clearer idea of who the Romans 7 man is. I strongly encourage you to read Romans 5–8 a couple of times over in one sitting. The message becomes clear when read as one continuous thought, which is the way Paul wrote it.

Chapter 5: Death in Adam, life in Christ. This chapter strongly distinguishes our old life in Adam from our new life in Christ. We are justified now by Jesus's resurrection.

Chapter 6: In light of Romans 5, we are therefore free from sin! We died Jesus's death with him and are raised in the likeness of His resurrection! We are not under law but under grace as new creations; we are compelled to live holy and obedient lives now.

Chapter 7: Paul now anticipated questions from the Jewish believers in Rome about their relationship to the law as Christians. Paul said:

> *"Or do you not know, brethren (for I speak to those who know the law), that the law has dominion over a man as long as he lives?"*
>
> **ROMANS 7:1**

This tells us he had the Jewish believers in mind now. He then explained we died to the law when we were wedded to Christ—a powerful and confronting transition for Jewish believers. To remain faithful to the law was to be unfaithful to Jesus. Paul then used present tense language to define his experience under the law, or perhaps the experience of Israel as a nation under the law. He knew the Jewish believers could fully relate to this.

He reasoned the law exposed and increased our sinfulness so we would recognize our helplessness without a savior. He made the Christians death to the law clear so the Jewish readers could fully embrace the fullness of the finished work of Christ and enjoy the new covenant.

> *"But now we have been delivered from the law, having died to what we were held by, so that we should serve in the newness of the Spirit and not in the oldness of the letter."*
>
> **ROMANS 7:6**

The context becomes clear now, as you can see.

Chapter 8: Paul could now conclude his thoughts on the law, summing up the subject of Romans 7 with:

> *"There is therefore now no condemnation to those who are*
> *in Christ Jesus, who do not walk according to the flesh, but*
> *according to the Spirit."*
>
> **ROMANS 8:1**

He then proceeded to unpack our life in the Spirit as sons and daughters of God, liberated from the law, and alive through our adoption as sons in Christ.

There are multiple positions about who the Romans 7 man is, once it is settled that he is not a Christian. Here are two popular thoughts about the Romans 7 man:

- Paul was referring strictly to his experience under the law. He used present-past tense language so that the Jewish believers could associate themselves with this past too.

- Paul was associating with the entire Israelite nation and its experience under the law, using present-past tense language still.

Either of these alternatives is possible, and I am not dogmatic about either. Few commentators are. The critical thing to settle is: Romans 7:14–25 is not speaking of the Christian experience.

When read through the right lens, it is incredible to see how we have misunderstood Romans 7. Misunderstandings like this have done far more damage than we have realized. For the church to live in the fullness of what Jesus purchased, we must remove such hindrances to holiness in our traditions.

Jesus did not win us in a rotary club raffle. He did not wake up one day and impulsively decide to redeem us. He purchased us with his precious blood: an eternal price with eternal ramifications.

God had all eternity past to anticipate our redemption and never thought twice about the cost. You are not a sinner anymore; it is time for your experience to bow to this reality as you embrace His righteous nature within you. He has seated you in His being; He has restored you from every hindrance that ever could have separated you from Him.

Do not miss out on your inheritance by believing lies about who you are. You are a blood-bought bride and must pursue to honor the price He paid. You can and must give the Lamb who was slain the reward of His suffering. Burn your Romans 7 sofa today. Come off the couch that may have kept you in habitual sin. Let go of the misunderstanding. Experience the liberty of truth and walk in the freedom you were purchased for.

(ENDNOTES)

1. See especially his Retractions 1.23.1 and 2.1.1: St. Augustine, *The Fathers of the Church*, vol. 60 (Washington: Catholic University of America, 1968), 101–4. "Against Two Letters of the Pelagians" 1.10–11, Romans 16:27 - Cited from Douglas J. Moo, *The Epistle to the Romans (The New International Commentary on the New Testament)* (Grand Rapids, MI: Eerdmans; Twelfth Impression edition, 1996).
2. Compare, for example, the commentaries of Cranfield, Moo, and Ridderbos on this topic.
3. *Strong's* G4560
4. C. H. Dodd is one of the strongest representatives of this view. Gordon College Faculty: www.faculty.gordon.edu/hu/bi/ted_hildebrandt/ntesources/ntarticles/gtj-nt/dockery-rom7-gtj-81.pdf
5. Calvin maintained v. 14 was not speaking of Christians, but v. 15 onward was. This cannot be proven though, and adds to the inconsistency. John Calvin, *Commentary on the Epistle of Paul the Apostle to the Romans,* trans. J. Owen (Grand Rapids: Eerdmans, 1947), 149.
6. Douglas J. Moo, *The Epistle to the Romans (The New International Commentary on the New Testament)* (Grand Rapids, MI: Eerdmans; Twelfth Impression edition, 1996).

CHAPTER 15
ARE WE SANCTIFIED?

Based on the message of imputed *and* imparted righteousness presented in this book, questions on the nature and process of sanctification have arisen for many people. We know now we are not on a lifelong journey from impure to pure—a slow purging of the old, sinful nature, only to be suddenly concluded at death. Holy Spirit does not share His new temple (you) with the old, sinful nature. He is not fighting it out with the old man in a lifelong battle, as though somehow the third person of the Trinity is only equal in power to the Adamic nature. To conclude this belittles Holy Spirit and is a misrepresentation of God. Just as Jesus is not unequally yoked, neither is Holy Spirit. A holy God only lives in a holy temple.

The depth of our relationship with God can be hindered or empowered by what we believe about Christian sanctification.

"THREE P" SANCTIFICATION

The view of sanctification most clearly influenced by the Reformation era (not discounting the influence of early Church Fathers) can be called "Three P" sanctification. This view can be broken into three main elements of sanctification. Positional (past), progressive (present), and perfect (future) sanctification. Here is a quick breakdown of each of these elements:

1. Positional (Past) Sanctification – This is the first step of our sanctification and it takes place at our rebirth. This is much like imputed justification. There are many Scriptures that indicate we are already sanctified (past tense). Theologians unanimously agree there is at least some form of sanctification that has already taken place (1 Corinthians 6:11, 1:30; Hebrews 10:10, and many more). However, this view limits it to a positional sanctification.

Because other passages indicate aspects of sanctification do not instantly occur (even positionally), we have to come up with suitable language to explain these. In this case, it's been labelled *progressive* sanctification. Positional language emerges. Common conclusions are: "We are both sanctified and being sanctified," and "saved and being saved."

2. Progressive (Present) Sanctification – Now that we are *positionally* set apart, considered by God as saints (but not *actually* saints), we embark on a progressive purging of the old nature, slowly conforming ourselves to the image of Christ with the help of Holy Spirit. The consensus is that death alone is the finish line of this progression. Passages used to argue this progression are valid (such as 1 Thessalonians 4:3, 5:23; Romans 6:19; Hebrews 10:14). However, the nature of the progression from the old man into the new man is misguided, as we have seen.

3. Perfect (Future) Sanctification – Eventually the progression ends with death. We have hopefully made progress in our sanctification as Christians through our slow removal of the old man, death to ourselves every day, and our fight against the sinful nature inside us. Our perfect sanctification then occurs, swiftly perfecting us by the grace of God from whatever stage we are at when we die. This is when we get our final state of perfection, our entire freedom from sin, and the sinful nature we never had access to in life.

You are probably familiar with this "Three P" concept, even though a variety of terms can explain it. A classic picture of "Three P" sanctification is presented in John Bunyan's famous book *The Pilgrim's Progress.* There are many modern teachers of this view. It is heavily influenced by the theology of Martin Luther, with arguments being largely rooted in Romans 7 as a key conclusive argument for the ongoing battle with sin and progressive sanctification. We have already seen this conclusion is flawed because Romans 7 (v. 14–25) is not referring to the Christian experience. I agree with Luther and modern teachers of "Three P" sanctification that there is a progressive aspect to our righteousness being *lived out,* as I have written about and will look at below. But this is not accurately reflected in an ongoing transitional process of sanctification from the old man into the new man.

Some who teach this "Three P" view do so to preserve the beauty of practical holiness, from some unfortunate excesses being taught in modern circles, leading people to complacency. They want to provoke a pursuit of manifest holiness in the church. I highly value the heart of this and share this same pursuit. However, this does not make the view scripturally accurate.

"ONE P" SANCTIFICATION

1. Perfect (Present and Future) Sanctification

"One P" sanctification skips straight over the positional and progressive sanctification ideas and believes there is only *perfect* sanctification. People who hold this stance strongly deny positional paradigms and paradoxes, reasoning our scriptural sanctification is actual, making it perfect; or nonexistent, meaning we are not even redeemed to begin with, removing all middle ground. They use the same Scripture verses used by "Three P" proponents that show our sanctification, but remove any idea of a mere positional participation, arguing it is as real in our inner man as the air we breathe and the bodies we live in. People teaching this idea are sometimes termed "modern grace" teachers, but the view is not limited to this circle.

By using compelling Scriptures like the following, some argue sanctification must be perfect, once and for all, at the point of salvation:

> *"And because of him you are in Christ Jesus, who became to us wisdom from God, righteousness and sanctification and redemption."*
> **1 CORINTHIANS 1:30**

This verse states Jesus became our sanctification—not our lifelong process, but our one-time setting apart. Where "Three P" adherents would call this "positional," the "One P" adherents call it "perfect," arguing it is unfathomable to limit the beauty of Christ's redemption to an intangible, unattainable positional language. I agree with this argument.

> *"For everything created by God is good, and nothing is to be rejected if it is received with thanksgiving, for it is made holy (hagiazō) by the word of God and prayer."*
> **1 TIMOTHY 4:4-5**

The primary Greek word used for sanctification is *hagiazō*. It means "to separate from profane things and dedicate to God," or "to purify by expiation: free from the guilt of sin, to purify internally by renewing of the soul."[1] The word used here refers to praying for food about to be eaten. It takes only a moment to "sanctify" our dinner, so why would it take a lifetime to sanctify ourselves?

> *"Do you say of him whom the Father consecrated (hagiazō) and sent into the world, 'You are blaspheming,' because I said, 'I am the Son of God'?"*
>
> **JOHN 10:36**

Now Jesus is referred to as having been sanctified. This throws real spanners in our theological wheels if sanctification is a progressive purging of the sinful nature that lasts until death. Jesus is eternally perfect. He did not become perfect at the incarnation; He always had been. He was "set apart" by the Father for a mission on the earth; this does not mean He underwent what we have believed progressive sanctification is.

> *"Or do you not know that the unrighteous will not inherit the kingdom of God? Do not be deceived: neither the sexually immoral, nor idolaters, nor adulterers, nor men who practice homosexuality, nor thieves, nor the greedy, nor drunkards, nor revilers, nor swindlers will inherit the kingdom of God. And such were some of you. But you were washed, you were sanctified, you were justified in the name of the Lord Jesus Christ and by the Spirit of our God."*
>
> **1 CORINTHIANS 6:9-11**

Again, here we seem to have been totally sanctified by Holy Spirit through the name of Jesus at rebirth, not through a lifelong process. We can see there is clear evidence for a real purifying, setting apart, and cleansing that happened when we were born again. If we remove the Romans 7 influence and positional thinking around these ideas, it can have tangible effects in our lives that need not take a lifetime of incremental attainment.

I see scriptural merit in this view. Many who oppose this idea fear this paradigm leads to sinful living and removes a pursuit of self-control and discipline. Certainly, for some, it does. I think this is sometimes more the fault of the hearers than of the preachers. Some people are seeking to gather teachers to suit their twisted, deceived paradigms. You can find an excuse to live in sin even in the most legalistic sermons around if you are looking for it.

The heart of a "One P" message is usually a genuine desire to see people liberated from self-effort and religious bondage rather than to encourage sinful living. However, I do not agree with all the methods or language of those who hold to "One P" sanctification.

This "One P" stance holds there is no such thing as progressive sanctification. I agree sanctification is not progressive in the sense we are slowly ridding ourselves of the sinful nature to become more like Christ, but let's now look at a final way of seeing this below.

"TWO P" SANCTIFICATION

You have probably guessed "Two P" sanctification does not start with positional sanctification, but like the "One P" paradigm, it starts with perfect sanctification. However, it has an equally critical second "p" to it, to bring scriptural health and clarity to perfect sanctification, taking this from intangible theology to a renewed, healthy Christian lifestyle.

1. Perfect (Present and Future) Sanctification – We must remove the misguided Romans 7 lens and the positional language that passages like it have inspired, along with the influence of our experience, which we may have given too much say in the matter. Only then can we see sanctification is perfect. It happened, not just philosophically, but actually. We have seen this in the argument of the "One P" paradigm. This is what it means to have been translated from the domain "of darkness into the kingdom of the Son of His love" (Colossians 1:13). It means you are "set apart." Your sins are "as far as the east from the west" (Psalms 103:12). "You were darkness, but you are now light in the Lord" (Ephesians 5:8).

The definition of biblical sanctification is that you are set apart. You were purified, washed, and cleansed from sin at the point of salvation, as we have seen in this book. Forbid your experience of ongoing, progressive sanctification to dictate the truth to you and submit your experience to the scriptural reality of your perfect sanctification. This is when *practical* sanctification kicks in, the second and *equally important* aspect of "Two P" sanctification.

2. Practical (Present and Future) Sanctification – Another Greek word for sanctification is *hagiasmos*.[2] it comes from the same Greek root as the words we have already looked at. The verses most commonly referred to that argue a progressive sanctification usually use this word instead of the previous word *hagiazō* (1 Thessalonians 4:3; 5:23; Romans 6:19). *Hagiasmos,* though, has more to do with us *living out* our perfect sanctification than it does with us attaining it to begin with. A misunderstanding of this Greek word, and our previous conclusions of Romans 7, have led us to our progressive idea of sanctification.

Strong's Concordance defines *hagiasmos* as "the *effect* of consecration."[3] It is the exhibiting of our already perfect sanctification. Because we are perfectly sanctified *(hagiazō)*, we must now pursue to *practically* express that sanctification *(hagiasmos).*

> *God is as concerned with us living out our practical sanctification as He is with giving us our perfect sanctification.*

God does not separate the two. You are sanctified perfectly on the *inside* *(hagiazō)* so that you can live sanctified on the *outside (hagiasmos).*

You have partaken of the divine nature, replacing the sinful nature, been set apart, and united yourself to Jesus Christ in one spirit (1 Corinthians 6:17). Now you are called to manifest your purity. This does not happen by slowly purging the old man; Jesus already did that. In the same way that Will the eagle became an eagle instantly, he still had to learn to function as an eagle, despite having been made one. In the same way, a human baby is born with everything necessary to be a functioning human and then he learns to use what he has. The baby does not become more human as he develops; he is fully human to begin with. For Christians, this growth happens by embracing the truth in humility and intimacy, growing in understanding, and staying in faith in the face of opposing circumstances or temptations. Then we will see increasing evidence of our perfect sanctification in our daily lives. We develop increasingly in character, maturity, and discipline, but we do not slowly put off the sinful nature and become more like Christ until we die. That happened at conversion.

> *Your sanctification is not something you are developing, but something you are discovering and learning to display.*

Let's look at verses commonly used to promote progressive sanctification, but with *practical* sanctification in mind instead:

> *"For this is the will of God, your sanctification (hagiasmos): that you abstain from sexual immorality; that each one of you know how to control his own body in holiness (hagiasmos) and honor, not in the passion of lust like the Gentiles who do not know God; that no one transgress and wrong his brother in this matter, because the Lord is an avenger in all these things, as we told you beforehand and solemnly warned you. For God has not called us for impurity, but in holiness (hagiasmos)."*
>
> **1 THESSALONIANS 4:3–7**

The word *hagiasmos* is translated as sanctification three times in this passage, and it always refers to practical living, not the state of our inner man. It does not represent a purging of the sinful nature but a purging of sinful *living*. This means God's will is that you would pursue living out your already perfect sanctification. Essentially, the message is, "You are an eagle, so don't act like a chicken!" Because of positional mindsets, we have previously concluded this passage creates a paradox for sanctification, meaning we are saved and being saved at the same time. We need to rightly understand the Greek word instead and see this is a practical term, not a progressive or positional one.

Paul compelled us to express our perfect sanctification by engaging in practical holiness, the expression of our sanctification—to live "set apart" because we are set apart. The same word is often translated for the word "holiness" and used in instances referring to our lifestyle and practices, not to our nature.

> *"I am speaking in human terms, because of your natural*
> *limitations. For just as you once presented your members*
> *as slaves to impurity and to lawlessness leading to more*
> *lawlessness, so now present your members as slaves to*
> *righteousness leading to sanctification (hagiasmos)."*
> **ROMANS 6:19**

The reason righteousness leads to sanctification is that righteousness represents your new nature and empowers you to live free from sin. This is not implying righteousness leads you to a slow and lifelong purging of the sinful nature, but rather a practical display of your already present holiness. You can see how this changes things, right? This is not a paradox at all. It is simple.

> *"But now that you have been set free from sin and have*
> *become slaves of God, the fruit you get leads to sanctification*
> *(hagiasmos) and its end, eternal life."*
> **ROMANS 6:22**

This verse says we are set free from sin and have become slaves of God. That means we are set apart, the exact essence of sanctification. This leads to fruitfulness in practical sanctification—the expression of our new holy nature in our lives as we grow in understanding and diligence in the truth. We need to change our minds from lies to the truth so we can live holy lives. We need to fight the fight of faith. However, we need not purge the sinful nature so we can become holy. God did this for us.

Our sanctification is perfect at conversion *and* there is also a process of growing in maturity which helps our practical sanctification manifest. Because we have put off the misunderstandings of an indwelling sinful nature, we are seeing people grow into this maturity extremely fast. I know people who have given themselves to a pursuit of this truth who live consistently transformed lives in a matter of weeks. It can be a challenge to embrace the truth, even when long-term feelings and thoughts are trying to convince us the transition has not happened in our nature. But when we stand firm in the faith, growing in intimacy with the Father, these behaviors fall away.

The process of growth in this paradigm is no longer restricted to a lifelong one. How long does it take to believe? How long does it take to choose the truth instead of lies, to choose intimacy and holiness? This does not mean you cannot fall from truth, fall into sin, or live in deception. This does not mean you can't be deceived and stumble as you are learning to express your new life. We must remain vigilant and disciplined in the truth.

Believing is a present tense responsibility.

The consistency, holiness, love, and freedom we can have is far more rapid and available than we ever imagined. I love watching the gospel work in people's lives in a rapid way. It is extremely satisfying seeing Jesus honored with radical freedom in people's lives.

PRESERVED AND PERFECTED

Saints are sanctified. In fact, the same Greek root used for the word saint (*hagios*),[4] is also used for the word sanctified *(hagiazo).*[5] This means the Bible could not rightly call us saints if we were not *actually* sanctified unless the sixty-plus times we are called saints is a strictly imputed or positional title, which is quite silly when you think about it. The Greek word *hagios* literally means "most holy thing, pure, morally blameless, holy one, sacred." That is quite a title! When we partake of the divine nature in our regeneration, we become saints. We move from dark to light (Ephesians 5:8), we are set free from sin (Romans 6:7, 18, 22) and we are made holy and blameless (Ephesians 1:4; Colossians 1:22).

> *"In the same way, a man can never be called a husband until*
> *he is married, a Christian can never be called a saint until he*
> *is sanctified."*
>
> **MITCHELL RAMSEY**

The reason the Bible calls us saints so frequently is because we have been sanctified. There is no other way to see this. We are set apart and have become saints. There are no varying degrees of sainthood. In the same way you cannot be 99 percent faithful to your spouse but cheat on him or her once a year, you cannot be 99 percent holy either. That would still just be called unholy.

> "Hagiazo ̄ is usually rendered 'make holy, sanctify, consecrate.' In the NT, this verb expresses the action of including a person or a thing in the sphere of what is holy in either a ritual (ceremonial) and moral sense. Thus 'to make holy' is to set apart individuals or objects for special use by God. Both individual Christians (1 Corinthians 6:11) and the church (1 Corinthians 1:1; Ephesians 5:26)

are sanctified or set apart for such service to God."[6]

MOUNCE'S EXPOSITORY DICTIONARY

Even *Mounce's* appears to boil this down to a conversion event, moving us from that of being morally unclean to morally clean. This is an instant transition, not a lifelong one.

Let's look at two important passages on this topic, showing you are both preserved and perfected regarding sanctification:

PRESERVED:

> *"Now may the God of peace himself sanctify you completely,*
> *and may your whole spirit and soul and body be kept (tēreō)*
> *blameless at the coming of our Lord Jesus Christ."*
> **1 THESSALONIANS 5:23**

When looking at 1 Thessalonians 5:23, Paul's closing benediction can appear to be a petition on our behalf for a sanctification process for our entire being. The problem is the word "kept" (*tēreō*) makes this impossible.[7] This word means "to keep, one in the state in which he is." It means to *preserve* a thing. How can God be slowly sanctifying us spirit, soul, and body, but still preserving us in the exact state we are in? Is He preserving us in a process? That is an oxymoron.

God is preserving us as *blameless*. Much like you do not preserve a nice jar of jam until you are content with the product, God has us in such a state that He now wants to preserve us in this blameless state and empower us to exhibit it. Let's look at this verse again in the KJV translation for a more accurate view:

> *"And the very God of peace sanctify (Aorist) you wholly; and*
> *I pray God your whole spirit and soul and body be preserved*
> *(tēreō) blameless unto the coming of our Lord Jesus Christ."*
> **1 THESSALONIANS 5:23 KJV**

You can see here this is more of a statement of our complete sanctification than a petition to God to complete our sanctification. When looking at a KJV Greek-English interlinear Bible, the tense used for the Greek word for "sanctify" in this verse is *aorist tense*, meaning you cannot decisively interpret it to mean it is an ongoing or continuous use of the word.[8] The aorist places no emphasis on the progress or length of an action, but only shows it occurs.

This verse communicates no process of purging, but makes a bold declaration of our sanctification and ends with the encouragement that God is preserving us in the state of purity. Paul was, however, making a request to the Lord that we would be preserved blameless. This shows there is a possibility of our preservation being hindered or affected. There is an active involvement on our part, the involvement of faith and our human will for holiness, which enables God to preserve us in a partnership with our desires.

PERFECTED:

> *"For by a single offering he has perfected for all time those who are being sanctified."*
> **HEBREWS 10:14**

It looks again here like we are becoming sanctified. Has God perfected us (made us complete), but we are also still being perfected (coming to completion)? This verse is often used to promote a positional and progressive case for sanctification. However, let's compare two different translations to see if it is accurate to translate the passage this way:

> *"For by a single offering he has perfected for all time those who are being sanctified (hagiazō)."*
> **HEBREWS 10:14 ESV**

"For by one offering he hath perfected for ever them that are sanctified (hagiazō)."

HEBREWS 10:14 KJV

Wow! There are extremely different implications coming from two reputable translations. When we look a little closer at the Greek again, we find the words "are being" were not found in all the Greek manuscripts. The language of process was favored by translators according to the traditional doctrine of sanctification and by their interpretation of the word *hagiazo* here. Now, note the statement the writer made just four verses before this:

"And by that will we have been sanctified (hagiazō) through the offering of the body of Jesus Christ once for all."

HEBREWS 10:10

Even the ESV translation presents sanctification as a finished event just a few verses earlier. So have we been sanctified by the will of God, only to be in the process of continual sanctification four verses later? No. To remain consistent, not just with the explicit message of our consecration in Christ, but with the context of Hebrews 10, the KJV stance on the Greek expression is more accurate.

For those who still argue in favor of the ESV on the Greek tense and expression of Hebrews 10:14, I suggest that in light of the explicit context of sanctification unpacked, this is not about individual Christians engaging in a lifelong process of purifying, but rather multiple people who are being sanctified as they come to a saving faith in Jesus at conversion. The expression for "those" and for "sanctified" are both plural in the verse's verbs, meaning it could indicate many who are coming to accept Christ and being set apart, as much as it could mean an individual in a process.

An example of this would be if you were seeing multitudes of sick people miraculously healed in your life. You could say "sick people are being healed." If I then took your statement to mean sick individuals are entering a process of healing, rather than many people being instantly healed, I would misunderstand your statement. When you look with fresh eyes, it is clear a case for the progressive cleansing of the sinful nature cannot be confidently formed from these verses, even though they are some of the most popular ones to do so from.

GROWING IN MATURITY

Am I against process or progression? Absolutely not. As we have discussed throughout this book, we are called to grow in maturity, discipline, character, understanding, intimacy, vigilance, and truth. The message of righteousness does not remove this Christian responsibility. There is a process of maturity as Christians. The key difference is we are not in the process of becoming new creations. We are learning to live life as the new creations we became when we first believed in Jesus. Also, this process need not take an entire life but is available at a rapid pace.

In Peter's second epistle, he painted an excellent picture of how we should pursue maturity and encourage others in this. Take note that just as all the apostles do, Peter preceded his exhortation to live a holy life, with an encouraging reminder of our holy identity in Christ as the root of it all:

> *"His divine power has granted to us all things that pertain to life*
> *and godliness, through the knowledge of him who called us to his*
> *own glory and excellence, by which he has granted to us his precious*
> *and very great promises, so that through them you may become*
> *partakers of the divine nature, having escaped from the corruption*
> *that is in the world because of sinful desire."*
> **2 PETER 1:3-4**

Peter introduced his letter with a powerful reminder of our identity: we have all things pertaining to life and godliness; we have precious promises granted to us; we are partakers of God's nature; and we have escaped the world's corruption. He did not stop at a beautiful declaration of our new life in Christ though. That would be wonderful, but impractical. His readers needed advice for their day-to-day life, and so do we. How should we live now that we have partaken of the divine nature and been set free from corruption? Should we just sing songs about it and encourage each other intellectually with it but live no different than before?

Peter answered this powerfully in the following verses:

> *"For this very reason (because you have partaken of God's*
> *nature, and you have all things for life and godliness), make*
> *every effort to supplement your faith with virtue, and virtue*
> *with knowledge, and knowledge with self-control, and self-*
> *control with steadfastness, and steadfastness with godliness, and*
> *godliness with brotherly affection, and brotherly affection with*
> *love. For if these qualities are yours and are increasing, they*
> *keep you from being ineffective or unfruitful in the knowledge*
> *of our Lord Jesus Christ."*
>
> **2 PETER 1:5–8**

Peter did not tell us to become new creations, become holy, or die to the old man. This was already accomplished in Christ. He said we must *add* to our faith the incredible qualities of Christian character listed above. He said we should not be ineffective or unfruitful in our knowledge of Jesus Christ. It is hypocrisy to have the language but not live a transformed life. We are called to increase in fruitfulness and effectiveness in our knowledge of our new lives. We are called to *exhibit* it, not just *verbalize* it. How do we do this without striving? We pursue understanding and intimacy with God. The natural response of knowing the truth and engaging with the Father, who loves holiness, is that we love holiness too. Then grace, empowered by Holy Spirit, makes these qualities manifest in our lives.

So what if Christians are not increasing in these qualities in their lives? Peter gave us a key reason they would have this deficit in the following verses:

> *"For whoever lacks these qualities is so nearsighted that he is*
> *blind, having forgotten that he was cleansed from his former*
> *sins. Therefore, brothers, be all the more diligent to confirm*
> *your calling and election, for if you practice these*
> *qualities you will never fall."*
>
> **2 PETER 1:9-10**

Here Peter gave the reason a Christian may live less than his inheritance and lack the qualities of Christian character. His reason was not that Christians were evil, deceitful, ungodly, or selfish people. He said a major reason someone lived in less than his identity was that he was "nearsighted unto blindness, having forgotten that he was cleansed from his former sins." Some have forgotten they were co-crucified and co-resurrected in Christ, are righteousness, were cleansed from their sin, are new creations, and were translated from the domain of darkness into the kingdom of light. They have lost sight of their identity (or in modern times, they may have not yet learned it). Peter's answer for this was an encouragement that his readers would confirm their "calling and election," meaning they would develop an assurance of faith in who they are now, as those called by God, to build themselves up in their most holy faith so they could live out their faith on the earth.

Peter then explained how he intended to help them in this:

> *"Therefore I intend always to remind you of these qualities,*
> *though you know them and are established in the truth that*
> *you have. I think it right, as long as I am in this body, to stir*
> *you up by way of reminder."*
>
> **2 PETER 1:12-13**

Sounds a lot like a Hebrews 3:13 culture, right? We should remind each other of the truth always because it is safe and right to be reminded. Believing and walking in the truth comes from living with a clarified view of who we are in Christ.

> *We must develop a culture that expects the qualities of Christian character like never before, but makes identity the means by which these qualities are empowered.*

What if we see people who claim this beautiful truth of their righteousness, but then live no differently than before, placing little value on actual freedom in their lives? I have encountered a few Christians who do not need to be reminded of their identity because they claim to know it already, but they are still living destructive lives. If they have no desire to live holy lives or to grow in character, then I suggest they have not meditated on and honored the truth in their hearts enough to pursue the manifestation of their new lives. They may not have learned to know the Father yet, which motivates this desire for holiness. This needs to be addressed in love, but addressed.

Alternatively, more dangerously, they may live with a seared conscience, as I spoke about earlier. Peter's method of exhortation, reminder, and focus on identity applies to those who are soft of heart, willing for growth, and pursuing the manifestation of their identity. If people are not in a place where they desire holiness or are excusing rampant sinful behavior with their theology, then they are in great danger and need correction from those who have access to them relationally or through leadership. I have highlighted consistently throughout this book that language alone means nothing if your life is not being changed or you are not walking with a soft heart toward God.

Your sanctification is final. Learn to live it to the fullest. Let your practical sanctification bring honor to God, who gave you your perfect sanctification for this reason. Let grace and love motivate you in every area of your life, learning to walk as a child of light because you *are* a child of light (Ephesians 5:8).

(ENDNOTES)

1. *Strong's* G0037
2. *Strong's* G0038
3. *Strong's* G0038
4. *Strong's* G0040
5. Precept Austin. "Greek Quick Reference Guide." www.preceptaustin.org/greek_quick_reference_guide.
6. Bill Mounce, "Can Jesus Sanctify Himself?" www.billmounce.com/monday-with-mounce/can-jesus-sanctify-himself.
7. *Strong's* G5083
8. Precept Austin. "Greek Quick Reference Guide." www.preceptaustin.org/greek_quick_reference_guide.

CHAPTER 16
A BRIEF HISTORY

Martin Luther (1483–1546) is one of my favorite historical figures. I love to study his life, and I am inspired by his persistence and courage. I often quote from his famous speeches, and reading about his exciting and history-shaping impact on the church has kept me up some nights. I honor him deeply. I also acknowledge his humanity. I try to consider his theological conclusions with other views that surrounded his in history, and the challenging context he lived in. After this, I find my ultimate answer in the authority of Scripture alone, something I know Luther of all people would honor, having given his life for this freedom.[1]

Martin Luther studied, interpreted, and translated the Bible with incredible insight in his day. But he did not *write* it. He was an inspired man but not an infallible one. God influenced him in his life and his achievements for the modern church, but he was not inerrant. Today, when he can sometimes be exalted beyond what is healthy for a man, this is an important fact to remember. Church history did not start in the sixteenth century, and Christian theology does not originate from the Reformation era.

I have left this chapter until near the end of the book knowing not everyone appreciates history, but for those who do, you will find this very helpful. I am far from qualified to write conclusively on church history. However, I have explored the historical progression of justification and righteousness theology in the development of Christian thought and will share some conclusions. Righteousness as an imparted and transforming reality is not a discovery, but a *recovery* of something misunderstood at a pivotal point in history, only presently undergoing a widespread change.

PROTESTANT PARADIGMS

There are figures in the early church who had a theology that the Christian remains sinful in his nature (at least in part). However, the modern reach of this paradigm among Christians finds its real thrust from the Protestant Reformation of the sixteenth century. Martin Luther, a key figure in this Reformation, had a lot to do with recapturing and reshaping Christian theology. He came to some conclusions about the nature of the Christian that many have since reconsidered, amended, or plainly disagreed with.

The famous conclusion of Martin Luther on the nature of Christians follows:

> *"The Christian is righteous and a sinner at the same time*
> *(simul iustus et peccator), holy and profane, an enemy of God*
> *and a child of God."*[2]

See the oxymoron here? A theological paradox was concluded. Luther appears to have been grappling with an experiential contradiction; namely, Scripture calls us righteous, saints, and holy again and again, but we can still have a strong temptation for and experience of sin. He felt this ongoing battle resembled our experience in Adam. He also had to deal with a misguided teaching of the Roman Catholic Church of his day. It was being taught that believers received an infusion of God's grace into the soul when certain practices were achieved, having to work in their efforts to appropriate and maintain a saving righteousness.

Luther countered this, as he taught that Christians received a saving righteousness instantly, by faith. This was radical in his day. However, he maintained this righteousness was entirely from outside us. He taught righteousness was merely imputed to us (rather than imparted into us) through faith, concluding it did not change the inner man. In combating Roman Catholic error, Luther came to his greatest theological recovery: that salvation was a gift of God's grace, through Christ alone, received by faith alone. I can't imagine what state the church would be in today if not for Luther's fierce and costly recovery of this foundational Christian truth.

Luther's conclusion about righteousness was that it was merely forensic. The Roman Catholic church's stance drove Luther to consider righteousness could not truly be tangible or infused, as this would cause works to appropriate or maintain it. Instead, he concluded righteousness must only be "imputed," or given to our "account." This meant, as we have seen, it was essentially a statement made toward us by God, the way He saw us, but not something that had tangibly changed our nature from a sinful one to that of a saint. Deterred by a reaction to the Roman Catholic opinion, Luther did not take righteousness to the degree Scripture taught. This has resulted in a Protestant terminology called "forensic justification," a paradoxical way of viewing the redemption of Christians.

Luther's conclusion, "simul justus et peccator," meant a Christian was at the same time both righteous and a sinner. Human beings were justified by grace alone, but they would always remain sinners, even after baptism. Romans 7 was the key biblical passage for Luther's conclusion of this thought. He believed Paul spoke directly of himself as "the Romans 7 man," rather than the more accurate, widely-accepted modern view that Paul was referring to the collective Jewish experience of the law or *his past* experience. Luther, however, decided Paul's conclusion of himself was, "Sin is his very nature; of himself he can't do otherwise."[3]

Unfortunately, this conclusion of Romans 7 has since been held largely in Protestant circles until recent years, as we have seen. This gives way to an identity crisis. When we believe we are viewed as righteous but still sinners, it proves difficult to consistently engage with God, due to a remaining sense of incompatibility. It also gives us far less expectation of a holy standard of living in the church. On top of this, it lacks the empowerment of redeemed sons and daughters, recreated in His likeness, to establish the kingdom of God. It causes us to conclude that when the Father looks at us, He can only see us through a "covering" of Jesus. Ultimately, the relationship becomes far more impersonal than God intended.

To put it simply, Luther concluded righteousness remained totally outside us as Christians rather than becoming an imparted reality. This was concluded from wrestling with the human experience of sin, a misunderstanding of Romans 7 and a possible reaction to the Roman Catholic ideas of righteousness, rather than by a clear and objective scriptural analysis.[4]

John Calvin (1509–1564) reconsidered Luther's conclusion. Calvin was a French theologian and pastor during the Protestant Reformation. He was responsible for the Calvinist theology held by many today. Some aspects of this paradigm include predestination, election, and the sovereignty of God. He wrote *Institutes of the Christian Religion,* a work intended to be a voice of clarity on the doctrines of Protestant reformers.[5]

Significant diversity developed among different reformers shortly after Luther's life as issues around Protestant theology arose. Calvin differed from Luther about righteousness. He proclaimed a union with Christ that was not just a forensic declaration of righteousness but a genuine transformation of the believer.[6] This is helpful to note. Other influential reformers, even some influenced directly by Luther's life and theology, saw righteousness as an imparted reality, not just a declaration of forensic righteousness.

PRE-PROTESTANT INSIGHT

The belief that the old, sinful nature is gone and we now share God's righteousness is no new concept. In fact, the "sinner saved by grace" conclusion is in some ways more modern than the paradigm of righteousness. Augustine (354–430AD), a theologian and philosopher,[7] had quite an impact on theologians of the Reformation, and in shaping modern western theological thought. He is viewed as one of the most important Church Fathers in Western Christianity for his writings. No sensible person claims his theology was perfect, but he is highly respected and celebrated.

Augustine believed righteousness was far more than forensic or imputed alone, but a divine attribute in which Christians tangibly participated. He believed it could only be obtained by God's grace as a gift (which Luther recovered and agreed with), but stated it was obtained and the person who had become righteous also became a better human being than he had been before.[8] Augustine used the word *justificare* to describe how we receive God's righteousness. This is made from two Latin words which he taught meant to "make righteous." He believed man was *made* righteous by an inner transformation that governed not only his actions, but also the motivation for those actions![9]

He went even further, reflecting on the fact that God told His people to live holy lives, saying: "I cannot doubt that God has not commanded human beings to do anything impossible and that nothing is impossible for God in terms of assisting and helping us to accomplish what He commands. Hence, human beings can, if they so desire, be without sin, if they are helped by God."[10] He even commented, when reflecting on John 1:12, "If we have been made sons of God, we have also been made gods."[11] This was his confronting way of expressing that, as His children, so fully partake of God's nature at conversion that we become the same substance as He is.

Other Church Fathers had similar comments to make, as they were confronted by these profound statements of Scripture regarding our new identity in Christ. Before positional or paradoxical thinking was a common way of handling the truth, they aimed to embrace the Scriptures more at face value.

Athanasius of Alexandria (296–373 AD), a renowned Christian theologian and Church Father, stated:

"For He was made man that we might be made God."[12]

Irenaeus (130–200 AD), who sat under the teaching of Polycarp,[13] who was said to have been discipled directly by John the apostle, stated:

"The Word of God, our Lord Jesus Christ, who did, through His transcendent love, become what we are, that He might bring us to be even what He is Himself."[14]

These influential Church Fathers believed in a tangible righteousness. Many prominent medieval theologians such as Thomas Aquinas, Alexander of Hales, Albert the Great, and Bonaventure, to name a few, also saw righteousness as an impartation of divine grace, and as it having a real and tangible effect on the believer.[15] For Thomas Aquinas, the infusion of grace involved a real change in the believer, who was set free from the sinful nature and given the ability to subject his mind and will to God. Aquinas considered this to be the equivalent of God's nature implanted into the soul, giving the believer an inbuilt disposition toward righteousness. Bonaventure taught that Christ had purged believer's souls of their inherited guilt, illuminated their minds by the example of His sacrifice, and then would bring them to perfection by giving them the grace required to imitate Him.[16]

There are many examples of pre-Protestant theologians who differed on Luther's eventual idea that righteousness was merely forensic, teaching it had an actual and direct transforming effect in the believer. More often than not, it has been seen as something tangible, not paradoxical. To be clear, I do not hold to all of the teachings or statements of these men. Rather, I wish to show here how dynamic and diverse our theological heritage is in regards to Christian salvation.

POST-PROTESTANT INSIGHT

So what happened after Martin Luther's life and the Reformation era? We already noted John Calvin differed in his conclusion of righteousness, but what about other influential theologians and revivalists?

John Wesley (1703–1791), who founded the Methodist Movement of the eighteenth century, also differed from Luther on righteousness. Wesley was also no Calvinist. He strongly opposed the doctrine of predestination and limited atonement, believing the gospel was for everyone. He also strongly emphasized personal holiness. Evangelism and practical holiness were two very distinct characteristics of the Methodist movement.[17] To prove Christians were not only called righteous by God but empowered to *live* righteously, Wesley said:

> *"I believe God implants righteousness in every one to whom He has imputed it. I believe 'Jesus Christ is made of God unto us sanctification' as well as righteousness."*
> **JOHN WESLEY, THE SERMONS OF JOHN WESLEY[18]**

Wesley had a belief in what he called "Christian perfection." He taught that Christians were so empowered to live holy lives that an "entire sanctification" could be attained, practically perfecting the believer. He taught righteousness was not only imputed but also implanted (or imparted). With this implanted righteousness, the believer could come to such a wilful, personal conviction of any sin that remained after conversion that finally grace would be stirred in the believer, who would then arrive at a state of perfection or entire sanctification.[19] This resulted in a removal of the propensity and temptation to sin so that the believer could be moved by love for God and others for the rest of his Christian life.

Interestingly, similar to Luther's heavy influence from Romans 7 in his conclusions Christians remain sinners, Wesley was heavily influenced by Romans 7 in his conclusions. Wesley believed Paul's description of himself as "the wretched man" in Romans 7 was the Christian experience, but only for Christians who had not yet reached the "entire sanctification," which he believed Romans 6 and Romans 8 alluded to. Romans 7 has caused huge theological debate and confusion over the years and remains so for many today. Wesley disagreed with Luther that Christians were both sinners and saints simultaneously, believing it not to be scriptural and that it would produce a less holy expectation and therefore expression for our Christian lives.

Wesley believed Christians could live free from sin when sin was defined as "a voluntary transgression of a known law."[20] This view has been criticized since. I admire that Wesley sought to scripturally explain the tangibly righteous life he saw evidence of as he studied the Scriptures.

William Booth (1829–1912), originally a British Methodist preacher who birthed the Salvation Army, also had an interesting case to make for Christian perfection or entire sanctification, differing slightly from Wesley in how this was attained.

There are other examples we could look at here, and I would like to write more extensively on this in the future, but the key points to take from this brief chapter, are:

- The language that the Christian is both sinner and saint, or a sinner saved by grace, has not been held commonly throughout church history, as we may have previously thought.

- Righteousness historically has been understood as significantly more than a "positional" or "forensic" statement of God toward us.

- Christians have been believed to be far more empowered in their practical walk of holiness than many modern Christians are being taught.

I am deeply inspired by all the men I have mentioned in this chapter. I have profoundly benefited from their passion and courage in pursuing the truth, as we all have. Despite having genuine honor for the man he was, and a high value for his impact on the modern church, I disagree with Martin Luther's conclusions of the nature of a Christian, as many have since. To conclude that Christians remain sinful in their nature after conversion does significant damage to the practical expectations we place on the Christian life and the relationship with the Father we are called to. There is a holiness available by recognition of a new and imparted nature of righteousness that is ours in Christ, which many are not experiencing and enjoying because of this flawed conclusion.

(ENDNOTES)

1. There are many biographies of Luther. A reputable one volume introduction in English is
Roland H. Bainton's *Here I Stand, a Life of Martin Luther* (Nashville: Abingdon, 1950).
Also Heiko A. Oberman's *Luther: Man Between God and the Devil* (New Haven, CT: Yale University Press, 1989).

2. Gerald Bray, *God Has Spoken: A History of Christian Theology* (Wheaton, IL: Crossway, 2014), 841.

3. Hans Volz and Heinz Blanke, eds., "Preface to the Letter of St. Paul to the Romans." *D. Martin Luther: Die gantze Heilige Schrifft Deudsch 1545 aufs new zurericht,* Bro. Andrew Thornton, OSB, trans., (Munich: Roger & Bernhard, 1972, vol. 2), pp. 2254-2268.

4. For a brief historical study on the doctrine of justification, or other historically developed doctrines, I recommend Gerald Bray's *God Has Spoken: A History of Christian Theology* (Wheaton, IL: Crossway, 2014).

5. John Calvin, *The Institutes of the Christian Religion* (Grand Rapids, MI: Christian Classics Ethereal Library, 1536).

6. Gerald Bray, *God Has Spoken: A History of Christian Theology* (Wheaton, IL: Crossway, 2014).

7. Michael Mendelson, "Saint Augustine." *Stanford Encyclopedia of Philosophy:* www.plato.stanford.edu/archives/win2000/entries/augustine.

8. Gareth B. Matthews, ed., *On the Trinity: Books 8-15,* trans. Stephen McKenna (Cambridge, UK: Cambridge University Press, 2002).

9. Philip Schaff, ed., "On the Spirit and the Letter." *Nicene and Post-Nicene Fathers, First Series, Vol. 5,* trans. Peter Holmes and Robert Ernest Wallis, rev. Benjamin B. Warfield (Buffalo, NY: Christian Literature Publishing Co., 1887), www.newadvent.org/fathers/1502.htm.

10. Philip Schaff, ed., *Nicene and Post-Nicene Fathers Series 1, Vol. 5* (Christian Classics Ethereal Library; 1.1 edition, 2009).

11. Philip Schaff, ed., "Expositions on the Book of Psalms, Psalm 50." *Nicene and Post-Nicene Fathers, First Series, Vol. 8,* trans. J.E. Tweed (Buffalo, NY: Christian Literature Publishing Co., 1888), www.newadvent.org/fathers/1801.htm

12. Athanasius, "NPNF2-04. Athanasius: Select Works and Letters." *Christian Classics Ethereal Library:* www.ccel.org/ccel/schaff/npnf204.vii.ii.liv.html.

13. Johannine Writings, "2. Polycarp's Teacher in Ephesus: John the Elder." *Christian Classics Ethereal Library:* www.ccel.org/ccel/schmiedel_paul/johannine_writings.iv.ii.ii.html?highlight=irenaeus,disciple,polycarp#highlight.

14. Alexander Roberts, James Donaldson, and A. Cleveland Coxe, eds., "Against Heresies (Book V, Preface)." *Ante-Nicene Fathers, Vol. 1* (Buffalo, NY: Christian Literature Publishing Co., 1885).

15. Gerald Bray, *God Has Spoken: A History of Christian Theology* (Wheaton, IL: Crossway, 2014), 516.

16. Philotheous Boehner, O.F.M. and Zachary Hayes, O.F.M., eds., *Itinerarium Mentis in Deum: Works of St. Bonaventure Series, Volume II* (St Bonaventure, NY: Franciscan Institute Publications, Revised edition, 2003).

17. Gerald Bray, *God Has Spoken: A History of Christian Theology* (Wheaton, IL: Crossway, 2014), 967.

18. Kenneth J. Collins, Jason E. Vickers, eds., *The Sermons of John Wesley: A Collection for the Christian Journey* (Nashville: Abingdon Press, 2013).

19. A large influence for this view of entire sanctification was 1 Thessalonians 5:23.

20. John Telford, ed., *The Letters of the Reverend John Wesley* (London: Epworth Press, 1931), www.wesley.nnu.edu/john-wesley/the-letters-of-john-wesley.

CHAPTER 17

FOUR THINGS THE "FINISHED WORK" IS NOT

I close this book with a final chapter of necessary balance. I have promoted the finished work of Jesus unashamedly. Showing the reality that Jesus solved the sin problem once and for all. He removed our old, sinful nature, making us compatible with the Godhead and enabling us to have intimacy with Him. It is the core message of the gospel. He has regenerated our essential nature to that of His righteousness, the same quality of righteousness the Trinity enjoys (2 Corinthians 5:21; 2 Peter 1:4). But it is possible to develop a "false finished work" mindset—a corrupt mindset that works against true freedom and intimacy. It promotes the death and resurrection of Christ as a denial mechanism for sinful lives and selfish motives, rather than a real deliverance from sin and death that has tangible effects in our present experience.

A false finished work mindset rightly emphasizes our co-crucifixion on the cross, but wrongly ignores the personal commitment to the manifest intimacy and fruit of the Spirit the cross purchased us for.

This can breed complacent Christians who do not live in the freedom from sin Jesus purchased but use the language of freedom. I believe this to be a very dangerous combination.

The finished work is the essence of Jesus's mission and message. If we miss the heart of the finished work, we will miss the heart of the gospel and how it applies to our lives today. However, we must also distinguish the things not included in this finished work.

To help us distinguish, here are four claims sometimes wrongly taught or believed about the finished work. The following claims are inconsistent with what Jesus and His apostles taught.

False Claim #1

The finished work makes practices like discipline, vigilance, and self-control irrelevant.

This is a damaging claim found in a false finished work mindset. The idea that because Jesus finished the work of our salvation, He also somehow lived this salvation out for us too, has caused many to live in a far lesser way than the finished work purchased us for. The truth is Jesus invites us to experience the reality of our salvation in our daily lives by our acknowledgment and steadfastness in the truth.

A beautiful element of our union with Jesus is we each retain our individual distinction while being perfectly one in spirit with Him. Jesus retains His soul (mind, will, and emotions), and we retain ours. At a personal level, from my soul, I now make a conscious choice to believe the truth and see it manifest. Or I can choose not to believe and continue living the same way I used to, even though I am truly a new creation. I am called to the *obedience* of faith (Romans 1:5). This calls for a personal decision to believe, even in the face of opposing thoughts, feelings, or circumstances, to see the reality of the truth become my subjective experience.

This is why Paul frequently used words like discipline, vigilance, and self-control in his letters. He told us to "set your minds on things that are above" (Colossians 3:2), "walk as children of light" (Ephesians 5:8), and "be imitators of God, as beloved children" (Ephesians 5:1). Peter exhorted us to "gird up the loins" of our minds (1 Peter 1:13), and to add self-control to our knowledge of the truth (2 Peter 1:6). These disciplines are our privilege to function from in life.

You may have wrongly applied these practices to grow in holiness or become purer, believing you remained a natural sinner after conversion. We know now we have already been purified and made holy through our union with Jesus. We now appropriate this holiness as our constant experience by remaining diligent in the truth. We must not throw out certain practices because they have been wrongly applied in the past. We must discover their redeemed beauty with a new lens through the finished work.

False Claim #2

A lifestyle of prayer and worship is unnecessary because we are in union with Jesus already.

I have seen people embrace a finished work message, only to disengage from a strong prayer life and a beautiful worship expression. Again, we must find the redeemed form of certain Christian practices, but not throw them all out because of a legalistic misapplication we may have experienced in the past. I used to worship God with the mentality that I was an orphan—not truly a full son of God. Because of my misunderstanding, I was pursuing a possible pat on the head from a distant God. If I had a soulish encounter during worship, then I would be satisfied briefly and reassured of His love for me.

Many of us worship thinking we are striving for God's attention, as though we do not already have it. Worship must be rediscovered now that we know the truth. We have wrongly made it a pursuit of a distant God rather than an enjoyment and a thankful celebration of the union we already have with Him in Christ.

As those who embrace the finished work, to throw away worship would be devastating. We are finally positioned to worship in spirit and truth!

Prayer, likewise, is something I used to understand as a groveling at the feet of a displeased God. Now that I know the truth, though, I can enjoy a deep and meditative prayer life from a place of perfect union with God. Prayer nurtures an awareness of His nearness. It is the reason the revelation of righteousness and the finished work exist so we can have communion and intimacy with God through a healthy prayer life.

Prayer is not just words you speak but a love you embrace and enjoy in various forms of experience. Do not let your past dissatisfaction in prayer and worship leave a bad taste in your mouth, leading you away from enjoying the thing you were purchased for. Discover what motivates true prayer and worship and get busy enjoying God. If you do not rediscover and enjoy these gifts of prayer and worship, you will be like those who win the lottery but never show up to claim the cash!

False Claim #3

If you have a strong focus on pursuing the lost and making disciples, you may be legalistic.

I felt the subtlety of this lie in the past as I looked into various finished work ideas. You may have heard a lie telling you you are unbalanced or striving if you have a deep hunger to see multitudes saved. I acknowledge some people have made an idol of outreach, wrongly finding their identity in winning the lost. This does not make a rightly motivated pursuit of the lost legalistic though. Again, we must discover what it means to be sons and daughters of God—free from dead works—who also relentlessly pursue the lost, compelled by the love of God and the liberation of the new covenant.

The heart of God never ceases to burn for the lost, but He does not live in an identity crisis, finding His worth in how many of His children have come home to Him on any given day. He is motivated by a jealous love, not insecurity or selfishness. Jesus came to seek and save that which was lost, but He was not legalistic in His approach. He enjoyed His Father, maintained a consistent awareness of His perfect union and acceptance, and saw multitudes touched from a place of peace, not striving.

This is our inheritance too. Do you strive in outreach or try to pursue the lost from a wrongly motivated place? Try closing yourself in a room with Father God and rediscovering His acceptance of you. Embrace His heart for you, first, and then for the lost. Learn to be compelled by none other than the same love you experience in that place of intimacy. A deep intimacy with God is the true fire that will see multitudes saved in our day.

False Claim #4

We are now free to enjoy all of life's natural pleasures, and to say that this can be a distraction is legalistic.

Sometimes we embrace this claim to redeem ourselves from Gnosticism: the belief that the natural realm is evil and we cannot enjoy what it offers, or the belief that the natural realm plays no part in our true spiritual existence and salvation, therefore we can do anything and it is not technically a sin. This leads to great destruction in people's lives. Many of us have experienced elements of Gnosticism in our past ways of thinking. We can develop an excessive idea that now we should have no limits or boundaries in the natural realm. Paul spoke of balance in this area when he said:

> *"All things are lawful, but not all things are helpful. All things are lawful, but not all things build up. Let no one seek his own good, but the good of his neighbor."*
> **1 CORINTHIANS 10:23-24**

Paul agreed Gnosticism is not something we should subscribe to. It is a dangerous teaching and had devastating effects on the early church, as it can today. But he also held that enjoying the natural realm as free sons and daughters does not transcend or replace the Great Commission and the purpose we have inherited of furthering God's kingdom and making disciples.

God invites us to set our limitations as a love response to Him so we can pursue the things dear to His heart and enjoy life on earth as His children. Both will equally bring Him glory. The things we previously thought were wrong or distracting, like loving coffee, surfing, eating great food, etc. are no longer seen as evil. But when we behold His selfless and relentless love for humanity, we develop an affection-based balance in life that cannot be formulated but is marked by a subjective temperance and missional pursuit. The key is being motivated by the value of others, not ourselves. When we do this, we find most questions in this area answer themselves.

FIGHTING A FINISHED WORK INOCULATION

Picture this. On a street are two churches. The first church believes and teaches Christians are sinners saved by grace. Because faith meets expectation, they experience their belief system and live well-meaning but limited lives. The second church speaks with the amazing language of the finished work. Its members profess they are "saints by nature" and "the righteousness of God in Christ Jesus." However, because they have believed some false finished work ideas, or used their revelation as a means of social status or contention, rather than intimacy with God, they are so blinded that they live identical lives to the first church, if not worse. They are satisfied with the language, but void of the love and freedom this language points to.

The first church is well aware of the deficit, however. This is how religious inoculation happens. People get wind of righteousness language and the claims of real holiness declared as possible by its preachers. But sometimes the message is not being lived to the degree the language is spoken. This causes people to disengage from the message and any hope of real holiness. Once this inoculation happens, even if someone comes along with a real manifest expression of the message, people are often hardened. They tasted the message from the other church but saw no fruit manifested in the lives of its people. This is a very sad thing.

The standard of righteousness has never been higher or more accessible than through proper understanding and authentic intimacy with God.

It is critical we live the message we preach. Will you commit to living in the holiness and authenticity of Jesus's finished work? Will you reject "false finished work" paradigms that lead to complacency or pride? They must be removed from our thoughts and platforms. They are more dangerous than we know.

We are called to see whole communities in our generation living with a manifest consistency, intimacy, and holiness, unprecedented in the church. As we stand for the truth in love, we can overcome the deceitfulness of sin and see the bride victoriously represent its groom, not just in small pockets, but globally.

CONCLUSION

I pray you have experienced the tangible reality of what I shared in this book as you have read. I pray you have engaged with Father God in ways you may only have previously imagined. I pray you are convinced of His goodness and love in your life. I pray you have experienced liberty from guilt, shame, and condemnation, and a release from any ambiguous hindrance between you and the Father in your life. I pray that your standard for the normal Christian life will never be the same.

It is one thing to comment on a significant event once it is already history. It is another thing to call something out in motion. We are in the midst of a historical awakening to the reality of righteousness, which leads to a profound intimacy with God, marked by real Christlike behavior.

Here are key attributes and values to look for in this awakening. These are likely signs the message is present in your life and in the life of your community.

1. All Will Know the Father

This is the main thing. First, we will know Him. This is God's greatest desire and our greatest desire. It is the aim of our lives, *to know Him and to make Him known*!

A corporate intimacy is emerging that will shock and intrigue the unsaved and saved alike.

- We are learning to host God in our lives and communities as those made one with Him.

- Extended times of corporate and individual prayer will continue increasing, as we come to such a satisfying place in the Father that we long to just be with Him.

- We will not use our revelation of righteousness to separate ourselves from the bride and start a new "camp" but will seek to know Him in the great unified way He deserves across the globe.

- We will use our revelation of righteousness for why it exists and *know the Father*!

Righteousness is the door. Please, never forget your revelation is only as good as the intimacy with God it produces.

We see increasing evidence of this in our Darwin church community. People travel here to enjoy our intimate atmosphere for a time and to be nurtured in their relationship with the Father and understanding of truth. Our life-on-life discipleship emphasis and high value for intimacy is a delight to be a part of. Freedom is infectious!

We see it in our Youth for Christ ministries, as people come from all around Australia to partake of programs like "The Jesus School," which holds intimacy with the Father as its highest value and emphasizes a proper understanding that leads to transformation. The power, love, and authenticity of the message is seeing many come to rapid freedom and knowledge of God in these programs.

The days are swiftly coming to an end when a Christian has more confidence to pray for a sick person in public than he does to sit alone in his home and have peace with God. Instead, the former will become the spontaneous love response of the latter.

If there is one aspect of the Christian life that should never be missing from our gatherings and lives in this generation, it is intimacy with the Father—the ultimate essence of the new covenant. Remember, to know God in a real way is not some elusive anomaly. It is not a distant hope, dreamed about only through a great divide of incompatibility. Our new life in the Godhead is God's greatest desire and most freely given gift!

2. Sound Doctrine

In the same way the integrity of the prophetic is under attack in our generation, so is the value and pursuit of sound doctrine.

"In all things showing yourself to be a pattern of good works;
in doctrine showing integrity, reverence, incorruptibility, sound
speech that cannot be condemned, that one who is an opponent
may be ashamed, having nothing evil to say of you."

TITUS 2:7-8 NKJV

I believe we will see a surge of incorruptible and reverent doctrine sweeping through the bride; a value placed on the truth that is unprecedented, uncorrupted by soulish and experiential interpretations of truth; and a Bible-loving generation—people who speak the truth in love.

- No longer will we be content to preach from our life experience at the cost of truth, void of tangible intimacy with the Father and true revelation.

- We will have real answers for real problems, finally, and a reason for preaching with a potent passion that transcends natural pulpit charisma.

- Ministers will no longer be defined by their doctrines, holding their positions in arrogance or with clenched fists.

- With open hands we will learn to discuss truth and gather around the Scriptures, defined entirely by the person of Christ, pursuing a unity of faith, with a real love for one another despite possible differences.

If knowing the truth sets us free (John 8:32), then let's get there together and walk in freedom for Christ's sake.

Spontaneous Bible engagement and a love for truth, from the newest Christians to the oldest, will be a shock to those who have not yet seen the reality of what righteousness can produce. Once you realize the Bible is the perfect reference for your real identity, you cannot put it down. This will be accompanied with a whole new standard of biblical literacy, motivated by a hunger for intimacy, not intellectual idolatry.

The message of righteousness is a revised foundation of the Christian life—an accurate understanding of the substance of salvation. As we have seen, it challenges and transforms much of what we have considered to be normal Christianity. Our lives now exist inside the Godhead. This is what Jesus came to welcome us into through His humanity. He has regenerated our essential natures to become the perfect righteousness of the Father, removing the sinful nature forever and making us compatible with God. Without our understanding and faithful engagement with this truth, we will never consistently experience what is already ours.

3. Evangelism and Discipleship

The two cannot be separated, but too often are. We are called to make disciples of all nations, not to just collect confessions. To make followers of Jesus, not orphans who once prayed a prayer on the street or in a meeting.

Evangelism will continue to increase, along with the powerful displays of God's miraculous goodness that come with it. But authentic discipleship systems will rapidly rise to an equal degree as we continue to truly see the value God has for people's growth and transformation.

The freer we become in our revelation of righteousness, the more we will believe we have the capacity and authority in the priesthood to dynamically disciple others into a relationship with the Father like the personal one we are nurturing. We will see radical discipleship communities all over the world place a huge emphasis on being known by the love we have for one another in the church. Our aim will be to see Christ powerfully formed in people's lives (Galatians 4:19), not just consistent church attendance.

4. Loving our Lives Not unto Death

"And they overcame him by the blood of the Lamb and by the word of their testimony, and they did not love their lives to the death."
REVELATION 12:11

Liberty from ourselves looks like something. To die with Christ looks like a life laid down to represent the person of Jesus in the world. We overcome the enemy by the blood of the Lamb, the word of our testimony, *and* by loving not our lives, unto death! There is a divine invitation to a radical obedience to the agenda of heaven for the earth.

"Righteous radicals" are covering the earth, going to the darkest of places, carrying the good news of the kingdom. Love motivates people in ways religion never could. We no longer fear death because we already died in Christ. We do not receive the message of our identity through an entitlement mindset, but rather respond with an *obedient faithfulness* to our worthy King Jesus.

We will shine brighter than ever before in the world as we walk in righteousness and know the Father. We will see communities confront governmental systems with a purity and love that is very evident, even in the face of serious persecution. We will see secular industries seeking God's wisdom from the church, as we put our ear to the Father's heart for the earth and make it known to all. We will see saints travel in droves to see millions saved in their local neighborhoods and the utmost corners of the earth. We'll see groups of radicals who have taken hold of the gospel in truth and burn to see it glorified.

Not loving our lives unto death is not limited to drastic evangelism efforts either. We will also see an incredibly selfless kingdom way of life growing in all forms of Christian expression. People who work desk jobs, make music, raise children, fix cars, or cut hair will function potently as salt and light in a dynamic and diverse Christian culture—all equally infused with the passionate nature of God and the power of a selfless, glory infused, humble, and obedient life in Christ.

Jesus is not a part of our lives; He is our life.

A CLOSING REQUEST:

I ask that you would take what you have read in this book and have a long, intimate conversation with the Father. Change your mind from your wrong mindsets and embrace the truth about yourself in the security of His love. You really are the one He loves! He sees you, knows you, and is thrilled by you. He responds to you. He desires you. He is near to you. He wants to spend time with you in intimacy as much as you do. Intimacy with you is not a means to an end for Him, but an end in itself. He is satisfied and moved by your attention and affection. Do not believe a lie of an emotionless or hardened Father God. Jesus proved He is just the opposite.

He has cleansed you from all unrighteousness. You are His righteousness now. Let Him nurture your understanding and change your mind about His perfect goodness and nearness to you. Sink into your compatibility with Him and never be moved. I encourage you to go to the Bible for yourself and develop your deep conviction of this truth. Remember, if I can talk you into this, then someone else will talk you out of it. Take it to Scripture and let that be the final authority in your life.

Finally, will you dream? Picture your family, your marriage, your church, your workplace, and your world with *you* in it. Picture it as you *now* see yourself, not as you previously have. What does the world look like when you are in it filled with the fullness of God, walking in peace and love? Remember, faith meets expectation. What does the world look like when you are so aware of Christ in you that everyone else is sucked into that awareness, and the person of God manifests everywhere you go?

May we dream again about what our short lives could look like as ambassadors of heaven. May we have heaven on earth in every area of our lives, so the masses can see the light and join us in the Father's kingdom.

As we all move further into the fullness of the gospel together, let's remember:

The success of our efforts to teach righteousness to the world will not ultimately be found in our ability to explain, discern, or preach the message. It will be found in the manifest intimacy with God and the fruit of the Spirit produced in our lives, Christian communities, and society.

This is your wake-up call.

Awake to righteousness.

Mark Greenwood

ABOUT THE AUTHOR

Mark Greenwood is a teacher and pastor at Glory City Church, Brisbane, where he loves building healthy Christian community and seeing Christ formed in people through discipleship and equipping. Mark is also the national training manager for Youth for Christ Australia and the author of *Saints by Nature*.

Mark carries a strong teaching gift. He is known for not only communicating profound revelation but also for creating an appetite in people to know God intimately for themselves. Mark is passionate to see intimacy with God become the fundamental attribute of the church in this generation.

Mark and his wife, Christine, live in Brisbane, Australia.

For more books, articles, testimonies,
or teaching videos from Mark, visit:
www.SaintsByNature.com

Made in the USA
Monee, IL
08 January 2023

24807549R00154